LAMINATED
WOOD ART
MADE
EASY

THE FULL-STRIPE PATTERN

STEPHEN CAREY

Schiffer Publishing Ltd

4880 Lower Valley Road • Atglen, PA 19310

Other Schiffer Books on Related Subjects:
Turning to Art in Wood: A Creative Journey, $59.99
ISBN: 978-0-7643-4204-2
Wood Turning, from Tree to Table:
Bowls, Lamps, & Other Projects, $16.99
ISBN: 978-0-7643-3335-4
Segmented Bowls for the Beginning Turner, $19.99
ISBN: 978-0-7643-4165-6

Designed by Justin Watkinson
Type set in Bodoni MT/Minion Pro

ISBN: 978-0-7643-4730-6
Printed in China

Published by Schiffer Publishing, Ltd.
4880 Lower Valley Road
Atglen, PA 19310
Phone: (610) 593-1777; Fax: (610) 593-2002
E-mail: Info@schifferbooks.com

For our complete selection of fine books on this and related subjects,
please visit our website at www.schifferbooks.com.
You may also write for a free catalog.

This book may be purchased from the publisher. Please try your bookstore first.

We are always looking for people to write books on new and related subjects.
If you have an idea for a book, please contact us at proposals@schifferbooks.com.

Schiffer Publishing's titles are available at special discounts for bulk purchases for sales promotions or premiums. Special editions, including personalized covers, corporate imprints, and excerpts can be created in large quantities for special needs. For more information, contact the publisher.

CONTENTS

To my wife Carol—for who you are and who you have helped me to become.

To my three best friends—Matthew, Timothy, and Daniel. I am so proud of you.

To Juanita Carey—my friend and editor. Thanks Mom.

To Matthew Bose and the Hooksett Public Library—everything a public library should be.

To Craig LaCroix—for your friendship and help with design.

To Stanley Avy and all high school wood-shop teachers past and present— Wood is Good!

Lastly, this volume is dedicated to the millions of basement, garage, and amateur wood shop owners across America who have always wanted more. Let the fun begin!

DISCLOSURE

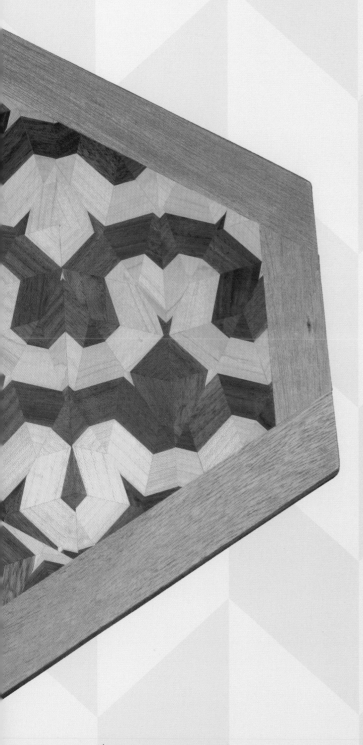

PREFACE

I believe it started back in high school. After English class in the afternoon, my classmates and I would enter the woodshop and find a world filled with power tools, wood, and a charismatic shop teacher. The focus was not on vocation, but craftsmanship and wood art, which captured the imagination of each student. Our teacher, a generous and kindly sort, gladly passed on his enthusiasm to his students. I won third place that first year for a lazy susan and second place the following year for a coffee table with a checker board insert. Over 40 years later, my own children play chess on that very coffee table, now in their grandmother's living room.

Some of the techniques and principles in that first shop class are here in this book. Others I have picked up in my 30-plus years of enjoying this fascinating and vibrant art form.

Imagine gluing different types and shades of wood together the way an artist uses different colors of paint. Imagine the wood grain displaying texture and vibrancy through those colors that only nature can provide. Envision combining those aspects into forms and designs whose dimensions and variations are limited only by the artist's imagination and time to explore them. Imagine multi-dimensional objects that can be picked up, felt, and used in everyday life—the round, the flat, and everything in between. I invite you to join me in this fun and exciting journey, exploring the creative world of the multi-generational method: wood lamination design for the home shop and hobbyist.

In *The Full-Stripe Pattern*, we will be covering a very simple design progression and scratch the surface of multi-generational concepts. We will take the time to cover in modest detail such topics as safety, jig design, tools, wood movement, moisture, and many other basics of woodworking. It is my hope that, with this foundation, you can develop the lamination design methods covered in these pages—and elsewhere—with confidence, and that this volume may become a reference for helping home shop owners and hobbyists accomplish far more than they had ever thought possible.

WHO IS THIS BOOK FOR?

Lamination: the process of combining material with adhesives to achieve a desired look or effect.

Cutting and laminating, or gluing, wood together for artistic effect and unique design has been a part of woodworking throughout history. With the benefit of today's improved tool technologies, this simple and fun process can become the playground for the average woodworking and home shop enthusiast.

We Begin with oak and cherry boards.

For example, above are oak and cherry boards, which are cut into one-inch-by-one-inch strips, as seen below.

Our boards are cut into one-inch strips.

Below we see a simple progression beginning. The oak and cherry strips are laminated back together into board form with a simple, 180° linear pattern of alternating oak and cherry called a full-stripe pattern.

These strips are laminated back together into board form with an alternating oak-and-cherry pattern.

Going a step further, we then cut our new laminated board at a 60° angle into one-inch strips. Next, we laminate them together again, flipping every other one to create a new board with the unique design seen below.

60°, one-inch cuts are applied to our new board. By flipping every other one, a chevron (CV), or zigzag, design emerges.

Above we see two generations. The first on the left is our original linear material cut at 180°, or lengthwise, along the edges of the board (a standard rip fence cut on your table saw) and glued back together into board form with a full-stripe pattern. The second generation uses 60° cuts across this new board, which are then flipped every other one and laminated back into board form with a chevron pattern. This new board is then used to create a lazy susan, as seen on the opposite page.

The new board, created from flipping every other 60° strip, consists of two generations (180°/60°) and is applied to the lazy susan (left).

This process is termed "Multi-Generation Lamination," or the "Multi-Generational Method." Each board is cut into strips, reoriented for a pattern, and then glued back together into board form. This process is repeated until the desired look or design is achieved.

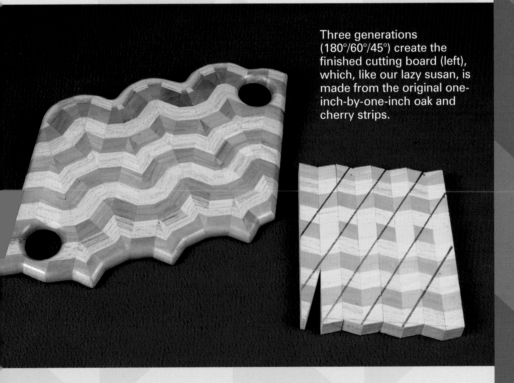

Three generations (180°/60°/45°) create the finished cutting board (left), which, like our lazy susan, is made from the original one-inch-by-one-inch oak and cherry strips.

Above we see a third-generation cutting board (180°/60°/45°) harvested from the same material used to create the lazy susan. The lazy susan's chevron (CV)/zigzag material is cut once again into strips at 45°. These strips are then harvested and laminated back into board form, creating this unique cutting board.

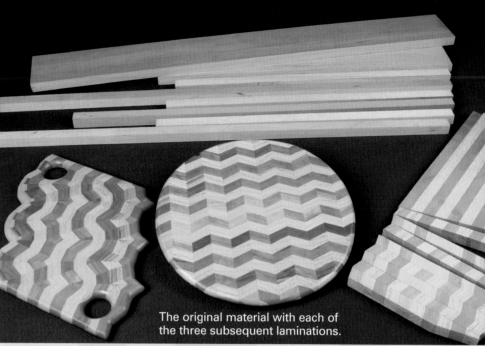

The original material with each of the three subsequent laminations.

Often when I speak with groups of craftsmen and hobbyists about the multi-generational method, the first comment is usually:

"Your designs are so complex; these projects must be extremely difficult." The ensuing conversation typically goes something like this:

"Can you cut a couple of boards into strips?"

"Yes," would come the reply.

"Can you then glue those strips back together again into board form?"

"Sure, anyone can do that."

"Can you do that in a step-by-step process, two or three times with the same material?"

"I don't see why not."

"That, my friend, is just how difficult it is."

Above we see our original material and each lamination displayed in order, clockwise from the boards on top. With each glue-up, we create a new board. From each new board, we cut and harvest the strips needed to create our next board or generation.

WHO IS THIS BOOK FOR?

My passion through the years has always been empowerment through education. It is my intention that this book be for the non-professional woodworker. Although professionals may find it useful, it is my hope that the majority of readers will find themselves in garages and basements across America. Average hobbyists are busying themselves with Christmas gifts for grandchildren and pushing the limits of their current woodworking skills to the next level. This book is ideal for clubs and guilds that strive to educate and inform their members of new ways to combine materials and discover new levels of their craft. In short, this book is about having fun!

Simple vs. Easy

My basement shop is called "The Broken Clock Woodworking Shop" and it revolves around the understanding that "even a broken clock is right twice a day." This is to say that, given enough tries, sooner or later we are going to figure out how to make a certain design or technique work. Often in the journey we find new avenues towards concepts and designs that we never would have discovered without experimentation. All the concepts and projects in this book are simple. They may not be easy (some are more so than others), but they are all simple. What is the difference, you may ask, between the *simple* and the *easy*? Oh, about two or three tries; meaning that if you are willing to stick it out, by the second or third try you will have something to be proud of, something worthy of a grandchild, a daughter-in-law, or putting under the Christmas tree.

Perfection and Production
vs. Enjoyment and Discovery

Why do you spend time in your shop? What is it about woodworking that gives you such a thrill? I trust it is not the potential to make thousands on some marketing website or having your work displayed in a high end art gallery. I have found that an insistence on perfection—woodwork without compromise—removes all the fun and enjoyment from our woodworking. Giving yourself the permission to get it wrong is usually the beginning of getting anything right.

This book is designed to enhance satisfaction and artistic expression in woodworking. It is not about production or perfection in woodwork. There is a time and place for uncompromising quality, but for many of us woodworking is our relaxation from the demands of a busy week, a venue of artistic expression for those who do not mind sawdust. Do not be afraid to substitute quality with enjoyment, or you might find yourself in your shop less, instead of more. Are you having fun? Is your shop time enjoyable? These questions are more relevant, in my opinion, than the quality of a glue line.

Learning Flags

This book contains different types of warnings, tips, applications, and variations that can be used while working with wood. These learning flags are divided into four categories: Heads Up, Tips, Applications, and Variations.

HEADS UP

Throughout the series I will try to give the "heads up" on different pitfalls and common errors I have encountered. They are here as a precaution to help you avoid mistakes and guide you through the more challenging procedures. When you see the red "Heads Up" flag, you will know it is time to pay close attention to details and safety.

TIPS

When you see the orange "Tips" flag, it will signify different shortcuts and suggestions I have encountered along the way. Included are suggestions to get consistent results, along with time and material-saving insights.

HEADS UP: (example) This is a very difficult cut and should not be attempted without proper safety equipment and guards in place.

TIPS: (example) Make sure your corners are free of glue squeeze-out before it dries or your next glue-up will not sit properly. I use an old toothbrush.

APPLICATIONS

This book is less about making some specific project and more about "making something to make something"—that is, making material you can apply to anything you can possibly imagine. A lazy susan, game boards, handles, a hot pad, trivets, coffee tables, cutting boards, napkin holders, platters, clocks of all shapes and sizes: all make great applications for your designs, which can be created using the principles in this book. Lathe work such as vessels, salt and pepper shakers, vases and bowls, and unique turnings are also applicable in both stave or ring construction.

At my website, www.WoodArt.com, there is a gallery dedicated to lathe work entitled "My Grandfather's Lathe" where many of the projects are applied to vessels and vases. Some designs lend themselves more to one application over another, but on the whole these concepts are applicable across a broad spectrum of applications. When you see the blue "Applications" flag, it will signify applications I have tried and others you might think about.

VARIATIONS

Many designs and techniques are like the tip of an iceberg: on the surface they seem straightforward, but underneath, there are endless possibilities. The type of wood chosen, degree used, or the wood grain pattern all may offer multiple variations, along with variations on those variations. There are endless avenues of artistic expression waiting to be explored with each generational design. When you see the green "Variations" flag, it can guide you in changing a design to suit your inspiration.

Safety is a subject we could spend the entire book on and still not have said enough. Common sense plays a big role. Have you read and re-read the operating manual for your power equipment? Have you taken proper precautions by clearing the work space and organizing your work area? Are your tools sharp? Another common sense question to ask yourself: "How do I feel?" Are you confident about this procedure? Does it make you anxious or hesitant? If so, it is time to listen to yourself and stop, turn the machine off, and unplug it. Take the time to turn your hesitation into confidence through education. Do not operate equipment you are not confident or competent to operate.

Glasses You Forget About

We wear seat belts in cars from when we sit to when we get out, because accidents are unpredictable. So it should be with safety glasses in your shop. The best money you can ever spend in your shop is on a pair of safety glasses that are so comfortable you forget you have them on. Whether prescription or not, they should be the first thing on and the last thing off.

Dust

Shop dust is a real concern and should be taken seriously. I use both a dust mask and a dust removal system. I have washable dust masks and wear them most of the time when I am working. Each night I give them a quick cleaning, and they are ready for the next day. At a minimum you should have a dust hose attached to each of your power tools (especially your sanding tools), leading to some type of dust collection. This could be as simple as a shop vac or a more expensive system designed for dust collection. Oneida® Air Systems makes some wonderful products, including the Dust Deputy®, a plastic cyclone device that mounts atop a 5-gallon

A collection of disposable and cleanable dust masks along with shop glasses.

pail or 55-gallon drum and attaches to any shop vac. It's a wonderful option for the shop on a budget. Also, I have fans mounted in homemade wooden frames and placed strategically around my shop, with cleanable furnace filters mounted behind the fan blades to help keep the dust level to a minimum.

Be Sharp

It is difficult to overemphasize the importance of sharp saw blades and tools when using the multi-generational method. Generational work often requires that cut strips of laminated design go from the table saw to the glue table. Any additional material removed by a joiner often results in noticeable gaps and breaks in the design.

When it comes to saw blades, there is no substitute for a sharp blade and the crisp, clear edges it makes. The sharper the blade, the cleaner the cut; the better the glue line, the better the finished product. I substitute blades long before they become dull. A less sharp blade will leave large and unnecessary cut and burn marks on the wood edge, which will need to be removed. This in turn may affect the design in a negative way. A dull blade must work harder to cut, which increases the friction level. Heat friction warps a blade, making it unusable for accurate woodworking. Having your blades sharpened locally is a great way to save money, especially if most of your equipment uses the same size blade. Generally my 10-inch blades cost below $20 each to sharpen, great savings when you consider their replacement value.

The Jig Is Up

Jigs could be discussed in every chapter of this book; I use them in almost every process. I handle jigs with safety because they add a level of comfort and control to difficult and dangerous cuts, and keep your fingers away from the blade.

What is a jig? A jig is a homemade tool, made to mechanize, simplify, or make safer and easier any project. Jigs offer a means of achieving consistent, accurate, repetitive cuts that allow designs to contain a higher degree of accuracy and uniformity.

A jig could be as simple as a push stick used with a saw or as complex as a multi-clamp, eight-foot hold-down ripping jig for putting a straight edge on rough-sawn lumber. Jigs can be used in all types of processes. Jigs are generally made of pine, plywood, or MDF (medium density fiberboard). They facilitate any process that requires repetition and accuracy.

I have a selection of push sticks such as these under my table saw to help keep my fingers away from the blade.

TIPS: Notice the small block with sharp drywall screws exposed in its bottom by a sixteenth-inch or so. This block is used as a push in the center of the surface of any board or material with the pointed screws facing down, holding the material firmly in place.

Glue-up jigs are a great help in keeping glue pressure even and holding your designs in place while the glue is drying.

Glue-up Jigs

Glue-up jigs are easy to make and are helpful in keeping your design lined up properly and clamping pressure even. A hard flat surface, such as a Formica® countertop, is essential. A true 90° corner is a must. Your newly glued board will only be as square as the glue-up jig that helped to form it.

A glue-up jig with clamps

TIPS: Products such as Anchorseal® and other wax paint materials that seal the end of boards and retard moisture movement are a wonderful way to keep your designs from becoming part of your glue-up jig. Paint your jigs and gluing boards with wax paint and nothing will stick to them. Wax paper is also useful in preventing unwanted adhesion.

Cutting Jigs

Cutting jigs offer much in confidence and comfort while operating your equipment. They help increase the quality of the cut while getting you and your fingers away from danger.

This cross-cut jig is one of my favorites for making difficult cuts. The use of double-miter gages improves accuracy and reduces unwanted movement.

Cross-cut jigs are simple to make using a hard flat surface and a 90° border on the rear edging. The use of double miters screwed into place adds a much higher level of confidence and accuracy, as well as allowing even push-pressure through the cut. Oftentimes the rip fence can also be used as a third point of contact to eliminate unwanted vibration and movement.

The handles of both miters help provide even, consistent pressure through the cut.

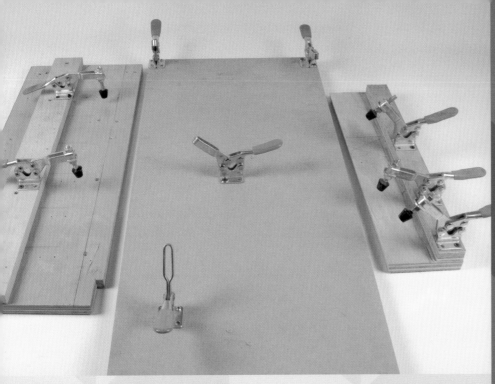

Rip fence jigs are some of my favorites because they accommodate almost any shape or size work piece and are easily adjusted with the rip fence.

Rip fence jigs are some of my favorites for their versatility, simplicity, and ease of use. The saw blade edge of a ripping jig becomes the line that can be used to align your design cut location. Also, they accommodate almost any size and design shape when held securely in place with hold-down clamps.

Sanding jigs are essential since much of our joinery comes right off the table saw.

Sanding Jigs

Sanding jigs are easy to make and play an essential part in the multi-generational process. Since we often cannot afford to remove material from the edges to make them flatter and straighter with a joiner, having a means to clean, flatten, and touch

TIPS: Note the "sanding clamps" in front, left, in the bottom photo. I find these "clamps" to be very helpful in maintaining a 90° orientation. The work piece is wedged between the round posts and moved across the sanding surface. The posts help keep the 90° orientation and also act as handles. These posts are also adjustable, sliding up and down, and are held in place by a screw to accommodate work pieces of any height.

SAFETY

up edges becomes more important. I have several, and continue to try new ideas to improve my glue lines and joinery. Having a very flat, hard surface is important, along with some method of maintaining a 90° orientation to your work piece.

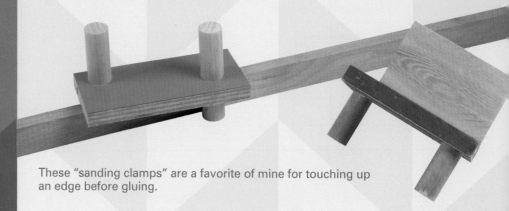

These "sanding clamps" are a favorite of mine for touching up an edge before gluing.

Making Jigs

When making cutting jigs, I recommend multiple hold-down clamps (found online and at your local woodworking store), along with peel-and-stick sandpaper or a non-skid-peel-and-stick step-tread purchased from a local hardware store. As the hold-down clamps engage, they force the work piece onto the sandpaper, which holds it firmly in place. Movement and vibration can be dangerous when making cuts, and a non-slip surface ensures a firm and solid hold between jig and work piece. Peel-and-stick sandpaper can be purchased at any tool rental store that carries floor-sanding equipment. It comes in grits 60 to 120 and is a handy thing to have around any shop. Many of my sanding jigs are made with it. Old belts from a belt sander and contact cement also work well.

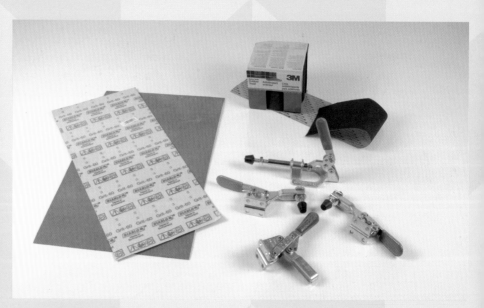

Jig making becomes easier with each jig you make.

Jig making and use is an essential part of woodworking. The more jigs you make, the easier and faster you can produce jigs, which give you accurate, high-quality work. The greatest benefit of making and using jigs is the confidence you gain, giving you a comfortable level of control while cutting.

We could spend this entire book—and a few more—on tools. In an effort to simplify, let's focus on what we're trying to accomplish and back up from there. As you discover projects you wish to pursue, your shop will grow. As resources become available, you will pick up tools and skills to speed up the process and improve accuracy.

Some of the measuring and layout tools that help make projects easier

Generally speaking, I purchase tools according to the tasks I am trying to accomplish and the projects I want to try. Another way of looking at buying tools is to use technology and your budget as a means of enhancing your shop experience. Ask yourself, "What do I hate?" and "What keeps me out of my shop or from completing a project?" These are the places to allow technology and budget to help make your shop time more enjoyable.

Cutting Wood

You will not be able to proceed without a table saw. Garage sales and Craigslist® provide a great avenue to purchase one on a budget, as well as Sears and all the "big-box" stores. My first table saw, on which I continue to do most of my work, is a 40-year-old Sears Contractor table saw with a 10-inch blade, purchased by my wife at a garage sale over 25 years ago. With a little adjustment, it cuts and runs true and is a consistent performer. Ripping and cross-cutting can be accomplished with amazing accuracy on any table saw if you take the time to properly adjust the settings, and make jigs to increase the saw's accuracy.

For cross-cuts, a miter box is handy. A 10-inch blade is more than enough. These "chop boxes" are nice and make miter work quick and easy on material where the blade will pass all the way through the width of a board. I did all my work on a table saw using jigs for 30 years and produced wonderful quality work, but I was delighted when I picked up a 12-inch miter box.

Flattening Wood

Resurfacing your work to a flat smooth surface is an important part of the process. A belt sander is a necessity as a means of making things flat. A 3-inch or wider belt sander with multiple grit belts is a must. These double as stationary sanders when a simple jig is made to house them upside down.

I use a 4-inch Makita Belt sander, with belts ranging from 36 grit to 150 grit, and have been very happy with it over the years.

Joining Wood

Since the lamination process involves extensive gluing, it is essential we spend time to ensure our board edges are straight and flat. The goal is a 90° orientation of the board edges to the board surface. A joiner is made for this purpose and is a great tool to have in any shop. A planer can also be used if care is taken or jigs are made to ensure the 90° orientation as it passes through the planer bed.

However, the first step in joining wood is making sure your table saw blade is set to a right angle, or 90°, and furthermore, that your blade is sharp and true, and that even pressure throughout the cut is consistently applied. This will ensure you get the cleanest cut your saw can provide and minimize the need for removing material with a joiner. Remember, removing material from a design edge will cause the design to line up improperly when combined with other segments. Your design pattern is the most noticeable part of any finished work piece, much more noticeable than the glue joints. In an effort to satisfy both, we must focus on the table saw cut and making it as clean as possible. In time and with good jigs and practice, producing joiner-quality cuts with a table saw becomes second nature.

Stabilizers, as seen in the image on the next page, are a wonderful asset for improving your table saw cut. Stabilizers are two donut-sized metal washers machined and balanced to improve blade performance. They are mounted on each side of the blade on the saw arbor, along with your saw's standard washers. These stabilizers help minimize vibration and friction, giving you an improved cut. They can be purchased online or at most woodworking specialty shops.

STABILIZERS

Two balanced, donut-sized metal washers, or stabilizers, improve blade performance.

Saw Blades

Without a doubt, the saw blade has the greatest impact on your saw's ability to produce the crisp, clean cut needed for the multi-generational method. Blades for this type of work should be a minimum of one tooth per half-inch of blade circumference, up to—and preferably—one tooth per quarter inch of blade circumference. Using π, or 3.14, we multiply by the diameter and arrive at our circumference. A 10-inch blade has 31.4 inches of circumference (10 x 3.14 = 31.4). A tooth every half-inch would be 62.8 teeth, or roughly a standard 60-tooth blade. A 60-tooth, 10-inch blade would represent the smallest number of teeth I would use on a project. Generally speaking, I like to stay close to 100 teeth in a 10-inch blade. Needless to say, these blades are expensive but well worth the money when you consider the clean cuts they make. Because they are expensive, I change my saw blade frequently, reserving my 100-tooth blades only for finer, artistic generational work.

Another major factor in getting clean cuts from your table saw is how the material is fed through the saw blade. Hesitant starting and stopping will give your blade and burn marks that will need to be cleaned up before you can proceed. A constant flow of the wood through the blade from introduction through exit will help minimize burn and blade markings on the edges of the board. An even pressure and consistency from beginning to end is required. I have been known to practice a cut several times—with the blade lowered or with scrap material—while applying even, consistent pressure through the cut in order to get the right feel for a smooth, seamless feeding of the board. To this end, I have found the double miter on my jigs to be of great help in applying even pressure.

Clamps... And A Word About Stress

Now that we have the means of making the edges flat to join wood, a wide variety of clamps will be needed to glue wood together. For smaller projects, I use rubber bands and spring clamps. I usually position bar clamps underneath my glue-up jig for horizontal pressure. On top I use a series of various clamps and wood-blocking devices for vertical pressure, keeping my designs as flat as possible.

There is a temptation among woodworkers to "make it fit." If their joinery is off a little, they force the joint into submission with clamps. I have found that this is a recipe for immediate gratification and postponed disappointment. Stress in wood is a lot like stress in people—sooner or later it will find its way to the surface like water finds its way down a hill. If you use clamps as a means of improving your joinery, sooner or later you will revisit the issue. Also, over-clamping can cause excessive glue squeeze-out, leaving you with a weak joint. In addition, excessive clamp pressure leaves clamp edge marks that can affect subsequent glue-ups. Consistent, even pressure is the key to uniform glue-ups and good looking glue lines. I think many of us would be surprised at the small amount of pressure needed to make a good glue line. I use rubber bands, among other clamps, because they seem to provide just the right amount of pressure, and increasing the pressure is as simple as adding more of them.

Gluing Wood

The most powerful tool in my shop is my glue bottle. Anyone can take one board and make two, but there is artistic genius in making two boards one. Lamination and the generational method, by their very nature, require lots of glue-ups. Having a glue-up table made just for gluing is very helpful. This table must have a very flat, hard surface that is easily cleaned. I usually spill out a cup or more of glue at a time on the table top and "dunk" the wood as I go. My glue table has all the essentials—glue, rubber bands, water basin, clamps, and a large, flat, sanding block to touch up the joinery. My glue is generally a woodworker's yellow glue that can be found in almost any hardware store.

Clamps of all types and sizes are a must. Any woodworker's "yellow" glue will do. Rubber bands give a nice even pressure.

Notice my belt sander mounted upside down in a jig for use as a stationary sander. The belt sander and random orbital sander (center, yellow) get the majority of my work.

Sanding Wood

Making wood smooth by sanding is a tedious job, but it is also a necessary part of every woodworking project. A random orbital sander is a wonderful tool and well worth the money, especially if sanding is not your first love.

Hand sanding and vibrating sanders work fine as well. This is another area where you will be glad you have a belt sander. With grits from 36 (very coarse) to 150 (very fine), they can really take the edge off a tough sanding project.

Sanding sealer and polyurethane are a great combination for a beginning finishing formula.

Finishing Wood

Here again, we could dedicate an entire book to this topic. My finishing formula is continuously evolving—it is more a journey of experimentation than a destination. Finish work is generally about three things: feel, sight, and protection. Your work will be judged by how it feels to the touch as much as how pleasant it is to the eye. Protection is another aspect of the finish. Finishing seals the wood and maintains a constant moisture content, which helps keep the wood stable, preventing movement that causes unsightly cracks and failed glue lines. This is why most pieces require upkeep to the finish as time goes on. It is also why they should be kept out of direct sunlight, which breaks down wood finishes.

TIPS: Notice the taller jars in front. A hook is installed to the bottom of the screw top lid, which allows the brush to hang free within the jar, not touching the jar bottom within the cleaning material. Cleaning the brush is as simple as giving the jar a firm shake after closing the lid securely. Also, the brush bristles remain straight, saving the brush for years of use. The trick is finding a jar tall enough and a brush short enough for the brush to hang a half-inch or so from the jar bottom.

TOOLS

23

A simple procedure that gets very good results, both in feel and sight, along with offering a good deal of protection, is using sanding sealer and polyurethane. I sand with 300-grit sandpaper or fine steel wool, and then apply as many coats of sanding sealer as time will allow. A minimum of three to four coats, sanding between each, gives you a smooth-to-the-touch-feel. I then might finish with a wipe-on poly, buff, and I'm done. If you use polyurethane, be sure to dilute it with thinner or mineral spirits. I have jars labeled with the percent of thinner vs. polyurethane (e.g., 50/50 or 30/70). Often I will use a 50% mixture for the final coat, then sand, buff, and wipe with a wax or oil product.

Food-safe finishes are also an important consideration. If you are making a cutting board, bowl, or food platter, it is important to stay away from potentially harmful finishes. Kitchen oils (olive oil, sunflower seed oil, etc.) are "food safe" and give a good look in the immediate, but tend to turn rancid and discolored in time. Nut oils can be hazardous to those with nut allergies. A safe and effective natural finish is mineral oil. Although it has to be reapplied every so often, depending on use, it gives the wood a rich finish and is completely food safe. Other food-safe products are waxes and oils found in your local woodworking shop labeled "Food Safe." Baby oil is another food-safe finish, which is essentially mineral oil with fragrances added. All food-safe products require maintenance on a somewhat regular basis, but give you the confidence that your woodwork is safe for food.

Food-safe finishes are also an important consideration.

I instruct anyone with a piece of my woodwork to keep it away from direct sunlight and radiators, and buff it with a wipe-on poly or mineral oil once a year (or as needed).

CHAPTER 4

MATERIALS

When I consider wood, in some ways I view it as a painter might view colors of paint. This "paint" can be expressed in a number of ways, but foremost in color and grain. For our purposes, we will be focusing on using domestic wood easily found within the continental U.S., with a few exceptions. As you can imagine, using "exotics," or wood found around the world, can open up a universe of color and grain, expanding your horizons of artistic expression.

Wood Color

Wood color can speak boldly or with subtle shades, depending on the complementary wood used and the desired effect sought.

I call this vase "EKG" after the lifeline image on the screen of an EKG machine found in hospitals. A large contrast was needed for this vase, so the maple on the walnut background was a good choice. The three-generation design material was cut into stave sections to form a cylinder (much like a wooden barrel), which then was used in the center. Several rings were added to the top and bottom to complete this vase.

This walnut and maple vase, or "EKG," is a 180°-1S/1"-45°-CV/AD-60° design.

These weed pots offer different color contrasts. The distinct contrast of the mahogany and birch on the left shows more contrast than the more subtle poplar and mahogany on the right. The center poplar and birch vase seems to find a better balance in contrast.

The weed pots above give us a good example of color contrast. The mahogany and birch on the left has a deeper, more distinct contrast. The poplar and mahogany on the right have a more subtle, less distinct contrast. The center vase seems to strike some middle ground with the poplar and birch complementing each other in a more balanced way. You may ask which is the correct balance or contrast? The answer: there is no correct or incorrect balance, only an artistic preference and individual taste.

The platters below are examples of "multiple first-generation lamination." It will be surprising to most folks just how simple and straightforward creating these designs can be.

These "multiple first-generation lamination" platters look difficult to create, but are quite simple and straightforward. Finding five contrasting colors for this project was a challenge, however.

Finding five different colors of wood that would complement each other for these platters was challenging. Contrast was the major consideration; care was taken to make sure each color held enough contrast with its adjoining colors. Below we see a more subtle contrast with this cutting board. The cherry, teak, and walnut complement each other in a modest way, giving this piece a character all its own. Its corners are of birch, which add to the quilting effect.

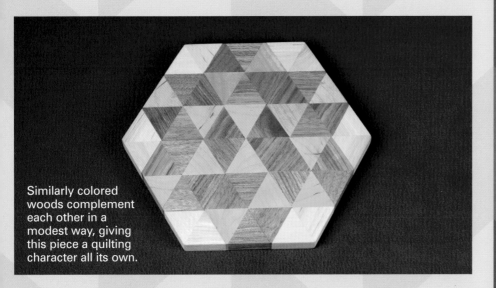

Similarly colored woods complement each other in a modest way, giving this piece a quilting character all its own.

The pinwheel design below combines both a bold contrast with a more modest one. The center is distinct, with a bolder contrast to highlight the pinwheel design. The exterior is a more similar cherry and walnut look, adding a frame (or bordered) look to the center pinwheel.

Experimenting with different colors in wood is fun and exciting. The objective is to combine wood color to compliment your artistic expression.

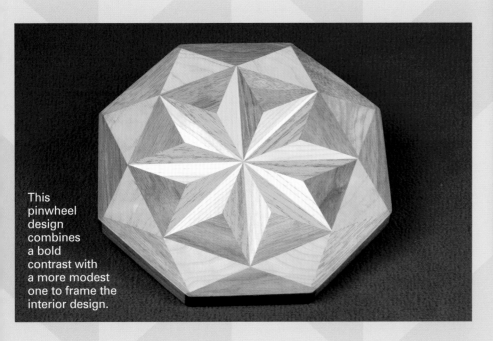

This pinwheel design combines a bold contrast with a more modest one to frame the interior design.

This vase uses the grain of the honey locust to speak boldly.

Wood Grain

Wood grain is another expressive feature that can be used to make unique displays and designs. For example, the vase above highlights this magnificent piece of honey locust's grain. The darker Brazilian walnut is less distinct in its grain and was chosen to contrast the wavy, sweeping grain of the locust.

This 6-inch coaster is an example of the use of grain orientation to create unique designs with contrasting grain.

As you can see from the above 6-inch oak star design, contrasting color is not needed to make wonderful, unique displays in wood.

Multi-generational laminations with the same wood species, taken to the third and fourth generation, can yield magnificent displays with no color contrast, such as in the 180°/45°/60°A/60°AD cutting board in white oak on page 29. The twisting and turning of grain orientation in the white oak speaks with an artistic expression all its own.

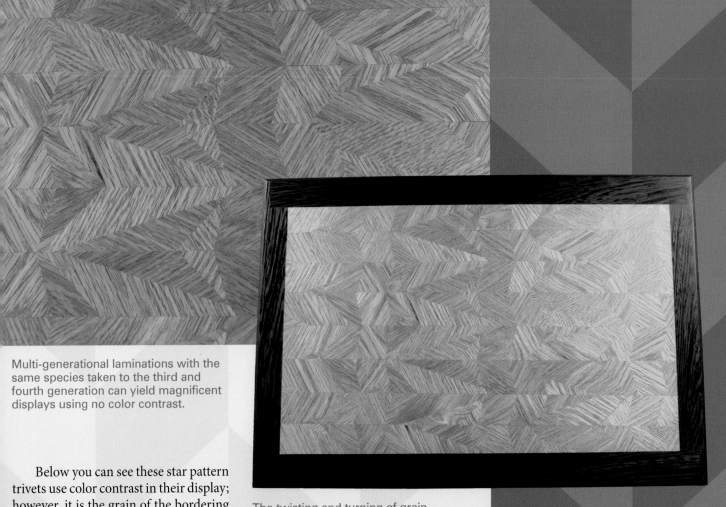

Multi-generational laminations with the same species taken to the third and fourth generation can yield magnificent displays using no color contrast.

Below you can see these star pattern trivets use color contrast in their display; however, it is the grain of the bordering honey locust that frames and augments the designs, bringing the piece balance and closure.

The twisting and turning of grain orientation speaks with an artistic expression all its own.

Using both color and grain to complement each other is an art form. With experimentation, each piece you complete brings you new combinations of artistic expression.

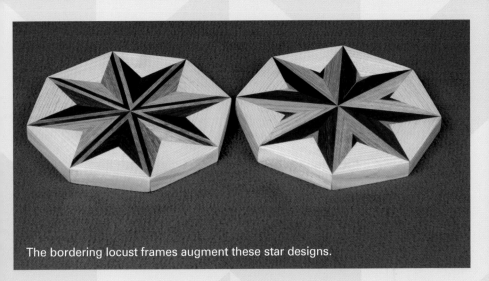

The bordering locust frames augment these star designs.

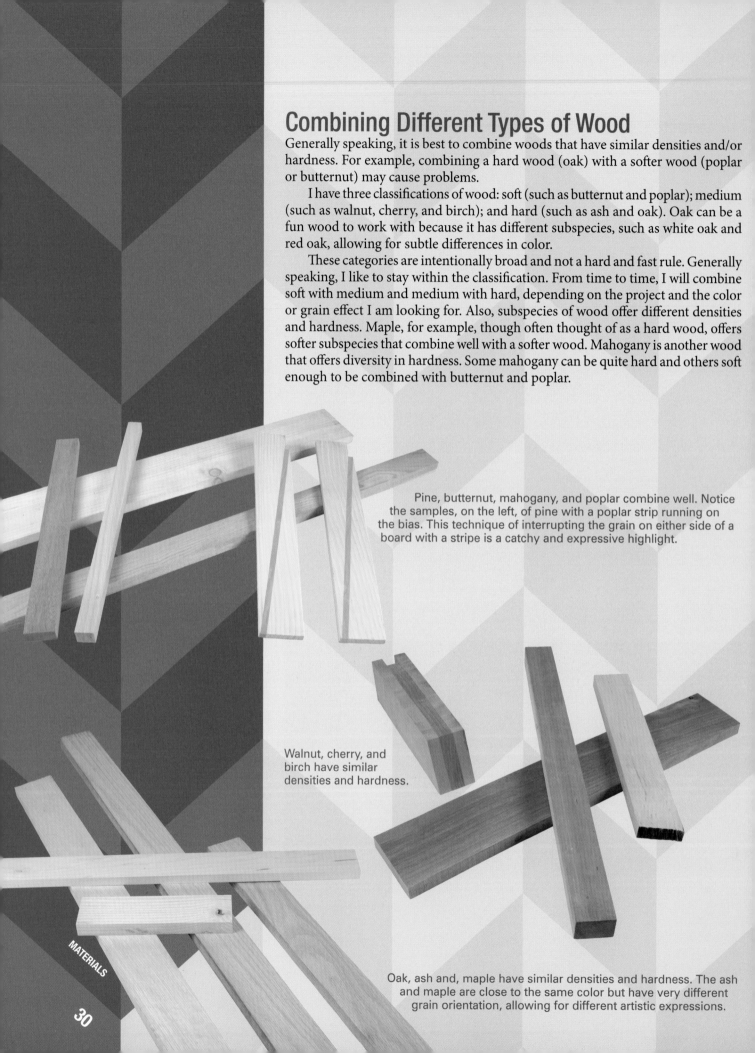

Combining Different Types of Wood

Generally speaking, it is best to combine woods that have similar densities and/or hardness. For example, combining a hard wood (oak) with a softer wood (poplar or butternut) may cause problems.

I have three classifications of wood: soft (such as butternut and poplar); medium (such as walnut, cherry, and birch); and hard (such as ash and oak). Oak can be a fun wood to work with because it has different subspecies, such as white oak and red oak, allowing for subtle differences in color.

These categories are intentionally broad and not a hard and fast rule. Generally speaking, I like to stay within the classification. From time to time, I will combine soft with medium and medium with hard, depending on the project and the color or grain effect I am looking for. Also, subspecies of wood offer different densities and hardness. Maple, for example, though often thought of as a hard wood, offers softer subspecies that combine well with a softer wood. Mahogany is another wood that offers diversity in hardness. Some mahogany can be quite hard and others soft enough to be combined with butternut and poplar.

Pine, butternut, mahogany, and poplar combine well. Notice the samples, on the left, of pine with a poplar strip running on the bias. This technique of interrupting the grain on either side of a board with a stripe is a catchy and expressive highlight.

Walnut, cherry, and birch have similar densities and hardness.

Oak, ash and, maple have similar densities and hardness. The ash and maple are close to the same color but have very different grain orientation, allowing for different artistic expressions.

These backgammon boards use plywood as a substrate; also, the surface area of cross-grain is brought to a thinner width.

Grain Orientation

As we begin to put wood together, it is important to understand that wood is constantly moving. If we put two pieces together incorrectly, they may repel each other in time, no matter how good our glue and joints. Since the key to wood lamination is glue and joinery, this takes on greater significance. Wood generally contracts or expands not in length, but in depth. That is to say, it will generally not get longer, but thinner or wider in breadth and depth, depending on the environment (moisture in the air). This motion can leave unsightly gaps and fractured glue lines. Many a masterpiece have turned into scrap within the first year or two, simply because allowances were not made for wood movement. What allowances? you may ask. First, do not combine segments of "running-grain" with "end-grain." Like the flow of a tree from roots to leaves, keep the grain running in the same direction, or as close to the same direction as possible. If you join end-grain and running-grain, keep it to as small a section as possible (generally less than one square inch of material). Planing to thinner widths also helps decrease the amount of cross-grain exposure.

When it becomes necessary to combine end-grain with running-grain, substrates help by affixing an entire section to a hidden sheet of plywood. The surface area of cross-grain is brought to a thinner width, like a veneer, in this backgammon board. I use this technique on my game boards, all of which are glued down to plywood before the sides and edges go on. Typically the finished surface is no more than one-quarter to one-eighth inch.

This 26-inch backgammon table is made of cherry and birch, with an oak middle ground, and uses a plywood substrate to help hold everything together. Whether your application is a coffee table or a free-standing board with drawers like this one, a plywood substrate helps keep everything in place.

This chess board
(2"-180°/2"-90°) is glued
to a plywood substrate,
then the cross-grain surface
area is narrowed by planing
or sanding.

This 24-inch chess-and-checker board is very popular. The red veneer accents the piece. Drawers on the left and right house the playing pieces. The plywood substrate helps to attach the sides and accommodate the installation of drawers.

These 180°/90° second-generation chess boards are a favorite of mine. After making many, I have yet to see one glue line fail or have a drastic grain separation. Note the use of veneer as a vertical accent. Remember that furniture-making essentials, such as dovetails, splines, and biscuits, are also useful in keeping joints tight and reducing end-grain separation.

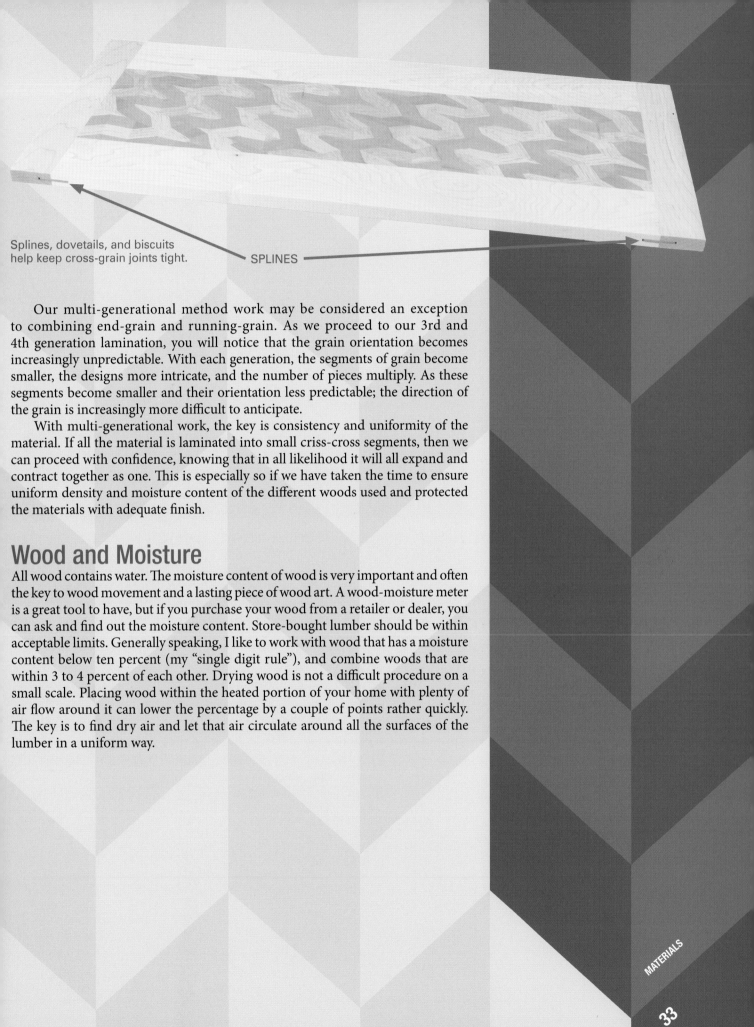

Splines, dovetails, and biscuits help keep cross-grain joints tight.   SPLINES

Our multi-generational method work may be considered an exception to combining end-grain and running-grain. As we proceed to our 3rd and 4th generation lamination, you will notice that the grain orientation becomes increasingly unpredictable. With each generation, the segments of grain become smaller, the designs more intricate, and the number of pieces multiply. As these segments become smaller and their orientation less predictable; the direction of the grain is increasingly more difficult to anticipate.

With multi-generational work, the key is consistency and uniformity of the material. If all the material is laminated into small criss-cross segments, then we can proceed with confidence, knowing that in all likelihood it will all expand and contract together as one. This is especially so if we have taken the time to ensure uniform density and moisture content of the different woods used and protected the materials with adequate finish.

Wood and Moisture

All wood contains water. The moisture content of wood is very important and often the key to wood movement and a lasting piece of wood art. A wood-moisture meter is a great tool to have, but if you purchase your wood from a retailer or dealer, you can ask and find out the moisture content. Store-bought lumber should be within acceptable limits. Generally speaking, I like to work with wood that has a moisture content below ten percent (my "single digit rule"), and combine woods that are within 3 to 4 percent of each other. Drying wood is not a difficult procedure on a small scale. Placing wood within the heated portion of your home with plenty of air flow around it can lower the percentage by a couple of points rather quickly. The key is to find dry air and let that air circulate around all the surfaces of the lumber in a uniform way.

CHAPTER 5

THE FIRST GENERATION

A 180° Full-Stripe Pattern

Creating the first generation is a fun and exciting project. It may become its own artistic creation, or we can continue by harvesting from it the building blocks of the second and third laminations to come. This initial full-stripe (FS) lamination is considered a linear pattern. It consists of 180° cuts, or a simple rip cut along the length of the board, which runs with the grain of the wood, to create strips 1-inch wide (1"-180°-FS). These strips of wood are then laminated back together into board form with an alternating pattern. This new board is *striped* by the laminated *strips*, and therefore, called a full-stripe pattern.

"Strips" are individual pieces of wood. "Stripes" refer to a design within a board. Generally, a pattern that is considered "Full-Stripe" has the 180° strips in a relatively consistent display across the entire width of the material. These strips will be alternating or differentiating in color or grain, creating a distinction between each stripe.

Whether a random or tight pattern, if the stripes transition over the entire width of the new board without bordering wider exterior pieces of laminate, it is considered a full-stripe, linear pattern. A full-stripe (or complete-stripe) pattern typically is completely made up of many "strips" of wood called "stripes."

We begin our first generation with boards of birch and walnut, which will be cut into one-inch strips.

We begin our full-stripe projects with boards of birch and walnut, each approximately four feet in length, six to eight inches wide, and three-quarters to one-inch in depth. These boards are then cut length-wise , with the help of a push stick, along the grain in a standard 180° rip cut, using the table saw's rip fence. The width of each board cut is matched to its depth and is approximately three-quarters to one inch. It is important that each piece's width and depth are equal, as this will directly affect our design. Since our strips have yet to be laminated into any design, we can use our planer and joiner to ensure these first building blocks are identical to each other. Cutting to a precise height and depth in each strip is critical in maintaining a uniform design.

Our strips of birch and walnut
are aligned in an alternating sequence.

Our strips of birch and walnut are then aligned in an alternating sequence of strips—first walnut, and then birch—while never allowing any birch strip to abut another birch strip or any walnut strip to be glued to another walnut strip. Having our clamps and equipment laid out in advance, and having everything in place and ready to go for our glue-up helps everything go smoothly.

Having our clamps pre-positioned and ready
to go helps things go smoothly.

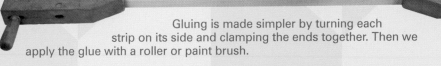

Gluing is made simpler by turning each
strip on its side and clamping the ends together. Then we
apply the glue with a roller or paint brush.

By turning each strip on its side and lightly clamping the ends together, gluing is made easy with a roller or paint brush. Once the glue is on, the clamps are removed. Each piece is then turned back to its original face-up position, and the clamps are reapplied.

HEADS UP: Using a push stick is important when making many repetitive cuts such as these. Keeping your fingers far from the blade will keep any "mistake" from becoming a trip to the emergency room.

THE FIRST GENERATION

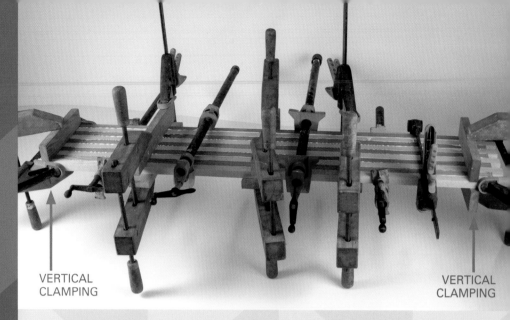

VERTICAL
CLAMPING

VERTICAL
CLAMPING

Care should be taken to keep the strips flat across the top, making our new board as flat as possible.

It is important for our new board to retain as much of its thickness as possible by keeping the strips flat across the top. To achieve this, we apply clamping pressure both vertically and horizontally, using blocking to maintain a flat surface. The resulting flatness will prevent a reduction of the board's thickness in a planer or with the belt sander.

Within our new board, the stripes transition over the entire width, and it is therefore considered a full-stripe linear pattern, because its width is comprised completely of stripes. After the clamps are removed and the glue is dried, our new board is cleaned with a belt sander or planer and it's ready to go.

At this point, we can go in two directions: either use this new board for a finished product (lazy susan, cutting board, platter, etc.), or harvest from this new board the segments needed to create another board in a second generation (or lamination).

Notice the sanding clamp and the sanding block. These are used to clean the edges of the new board, while taking care to ensure that no large amount of material is removed from the exterior strips that created our new board. If any strip is narrower in width than the others, it may throw off our design in any subsequent laminations, as we match one segment with another. This is not a concern if we opt for our full-stripe pattern to be our finished product.

Our new board after the glue is cleaned off. If the stripes transition over the width of the new board, it is considered a full- (or complete-) stripe linear pattern, because its width is comprised completely of stripes.

Simple, Single-Generation, Full-Stripe (FS) Projects

These single-generation, 180° linear laminations make wonderful, artistic projects anyone would be proud to have in their home. They are simple and fun to make. They also do not require excessively long periods of time in the shop to complete. This design celebrates the adage "less is more." With a design that is less complex, wood color, grain, and characteristics are highlighted.

Lazy Susan with Napkin Holder and Salt & Pepper Shakers

This lazy susan made from a simple half-inch linear laminate of mahogany and birch (0.5"-180°) is a favorite of mine. The designation 0.5"-180° refers to the width in inches for each cut, or what is called the "cut location"; in this case, every half-inch. A napkin holder is formed by a tongue cut into the bottom of the uprights, and a router is used to form a groove in the base to house the tongue. Screws are used to hold the uprights in place from underneath. A pair of salt and pepper shakers of the same material can be turned on the lathe. The lazy susan hardware can be purchased in any hardware store and is simple to install.

Simple Serving Tray

This simple serving tray of ash and Brazilian walnut is easy to make and elegant in its simple design.

This lazy susan is a very simple first-generation design with matching napkin holders attached to its center, along with a pair of salt and pepper shakers of the same material turned on the lathe.

VARIATIONS: The number of stripes and their color and width add a lot to this linear laminate design. More stripes and/or thinner stripes add a more complex display. A single center stripe of darker material, such as ebony, stands out and can make a huge accent.

Sadie's Cutting Board

"Sadie's Cutting Board" is another well-balanced pattern of 180° linear laminate. Cutting boards made from random widths in the scrap bin are a favorite at Christmastime.

Cutting Board

This cutting board is one of our favorites in the kitchen. It was a created with nothing more than wood from my scrap bin cut into strips of random widths and laminated together. This random pattern is another design with endless artistic possibilities.

Applying a 45° Cut

We begin our second-generation lamination with the material we have created in Chapter 5 (1"-180°-FS). Our laminated board, consisting of strips of alternating birch and walnut (approximately four feet in length and 12 inches in width) will be harvested into strips. These harvested strips are one inch wide, cut at a 45° angle (1"-45°), and they will be used to create new, exciting designs.

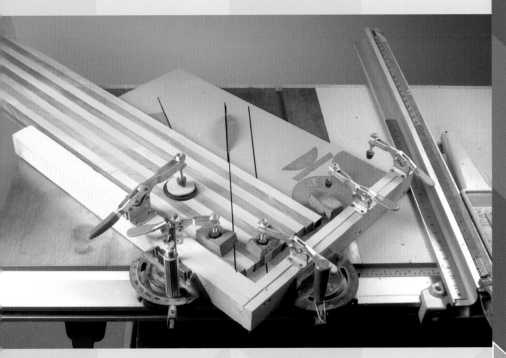

Our first cut is to remove the end of the board. This triangle is what I refer to as the "ear" and becomes the stop block for our jig.

Since our material is wider (12 inches +/-), we are confined to the table saw for our cuts rather than a miter saw or chop box. Fortunately, our cross-cut table saw jig will give us the accuracy needed to make complex designs. If our material were narrower, a mitre box or chop saw would be a good choice. Our first cut will remove the end of the board. This triangle is what I refer to as the "ear" and becomes an important part of the cutting process. It also can be harvested for smaller strips. Hold-down clamps and peel-and-stick sandpaper help ensure a smooth pass through the saw blade.

TIPS: Note that the jig has three points of contact with your saw, which help make this difficult cut manageable and smooth. Two miters sliding in their tracks and the rip fence give this process greater stability and accuracy.

Hold-down clamps help hold everything in place during the cut. Turning the saw off between each cut *before the jig is drawn back across the blade* increases safety and helps ensure a good product.

The ear is used as a stop block to ensure our cuts are all precisely the same one-inch width and is held in place by hold-down claps. The two sliding saw miters attached to the jig give us a nice even cut and the rip fence is brought in to help stabilize the jig.

Two hands and even pressure on the two miters, along with the rip fence, help make for an even, clean cut. The saw is turned off between each cut and each strip is examined for cut or burn marks.

HEADS UP: In the photo on top, notice how the hold-down clamps secure a piece of quarter-inch plywood over the cut-piece area. This small safety feature ensures that your cut piece will not "kick back" once it is cut free from the longer board. From the beginning to the end of your cut, nothing should slide, move, or vibrate out of position.

TIPS: Here we see the benefits of working with boards four feet or smaller. Generally, I will not create boards longer than four feet, because they are difficult to manage in a cross-cut jig. Longer boards in a cross-cut jig tend to make a cut unbalanced, resulting in saw and burn marks. Better to create two boards of four feet than try to move an eight-foot board across your saw bed.

The board is reconstructed and cut burrs are removed with light sanding. Each piece is labeled, examined for blade and burn marks, and placed in the order of the original board. If a particular piece or strip is damaged, marred, dented, or burned by my saw blade in a way that may affect the design, it should be discarded.

Each cut strip is inspected. Cut burrs and loose sawdust are removed with light sanding. The board is reconstructed and labeled with numbers clearly marking each segment's position in the original board on both ends of the same side. This labeling will give you the ability to experiment with different designs and shapes and easily find your way back to where you started. Also, it helps with aligning grain orientation. If, for example, your pattern uses grain to augment your design, aligning "piece number one" with "number two" would give you a more consistent, flowing look than aligning it with "number 27." By placing your markings on one side only, it is easy to determine which sections have been flipped over.

The process of experimenting with our new segments is a fun and exciting one. There are a multitude of combinations and variations available to us. With our new pieces we can begin to experiment with different designs and combinations to determine what our final project will look like.

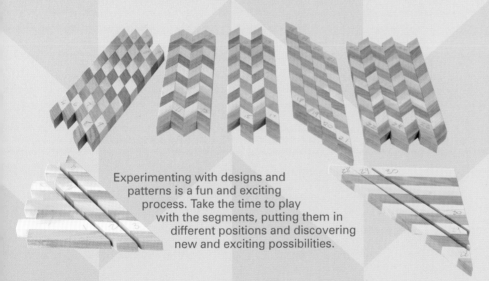

Experimenting with designs and patterns is a fun and exciting process. Take the time to play with the segments, putting them in different positions and discovering new and exciting possibilities.

Above we see only a portion of the possibilities. The bottom left and right are our "ears" from the original board. On the top, we see, from left to right, the diamond design (DM), the chevron design (CV, also called a zigzag pattern), the herringbone design (HB), a half-step diamond design (0.5DM), and a half-step chevron design (0.5CV).

HEADS UP: It is important to turn the saw off between each cut **before it is drawn back across the blade.** Manipulating the piece, removing the cut clamps, removing the material back into position, and re-clamping the material in its new position requires concentration and focus. Turning off your saw will give you the confidence that each cut is precise and that you are out of harm's way. Also, by not drawing back with the blade moving, we reduce cut and burn marks.

TIPS: Burrs and sawdust can keep a glue-up from sitting just right. Remove any obstructions with a light sanding, being sure not to remove any large amount of material from the sides, as this may affect the design in a negative way. This will also give you the opportunity to inspect each cut section for abnormalities such as burn and cut marks, which may also affect the design.

VARIATIONS: Experimenting with designs and patterns is a fun and exciting process. It is hard to illustrate all the varied possibilities available with these segments. Take the time to play with the segments, putting them in different positions and discovering new and exciting possibilities before you move on to the next generation.

The orientation of the cut strips together, and the display they create, is a wonderful field of study. For example, notice that, by simply turning over every other strip, we see the marked difference between the diamond and the herringbone designs; also notice that the common checker board design is the herringbone pattern applied to a 90° cut, rather than the 45° cut.

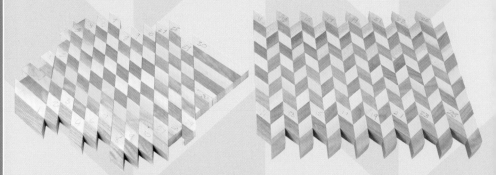

The designs: a diamond-design platter on the left and a herringbone-design lazy susan on the right. Use a magnifying glass to ensure proper alignment, and make markings before glue-up to help align the design properly.

After playing with these segments for some time, I have decided on two different shapes and designs. A diamond design (DM, left) will be used to make an octagonal lazy susan; and on the right, a herringbone pattern (HB, right) will be used to make a rectangular serving tray.

The Diamond Lazy Susan: a 1"-180°-FS/1"-45°-DM Design

Our lazy susan is a diamond pattern (DM). This design is achieved without any flipping of segments. Rather, they are aligned point-for-point so that a diamond pattern emerges from top to bottom. The smaller segments from the ears can be used with this lazy susan since it is round, or technically, octagonal, in shape.

Choosing a shape for our lazy susan that augments and complements its design is an important consideration. This often can make the difference between a good result and a great result. First, the center in relation to the design must be found. From the center, we can then begin to map out where a potential shape might be located. Once we have located the center, we can begin to draw different shapes on our project to see how they may complement the design.

Below we see a circle and an octagon drawn on the lazy susan. The octagonal shape complements the diamonds better and gives a symmetrical, balanced look to our lazy susan. Also, it seems to give it enough usable surface space to be practical on any kitchen table.

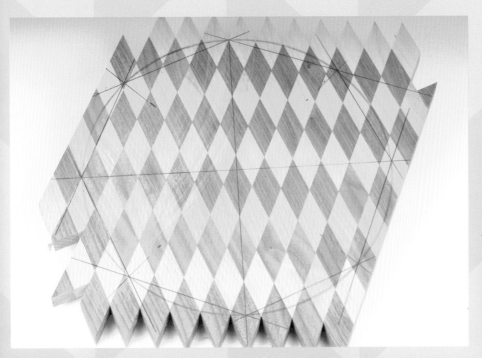

Choosing a shape that accents your design can be the difference between a good result and a great result.

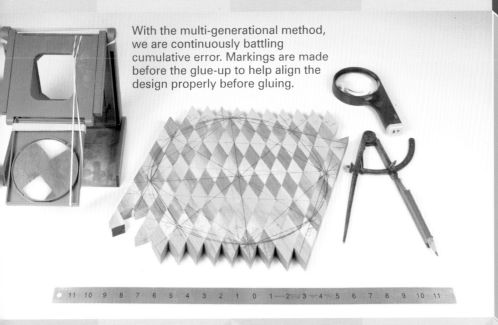

With the multi-generational method, we are continuously battling cumulative error. Markings are made before the glue-up to help align the design properly before gluing.

Before gluing, it is essential that the design is aligned as precisely as possible. I use a magnifying glass to aid me in this process. Until I know they are as close to being uniform as possible, I will not proceed. Once they are precisely where I want them to be, lines are drawn and markings made so that during glue-up, getting them back into precise position is as simple as realigning the markings.

TIPS: A magnifying glass is a must for this type of work. With each generation, we battle against cumulative error. If a line is off by a 64th of an inch in the first generation, it will become a quarter-inch gap in the fourth. Keep your designs tight throughout your work and your fourth and fifth generations will show it.

TIPS: Notice the ruler in this photo. Markings begin in the center, at "0," and move out 12 inches to both the left and right. This simple tool is a great asset and huge time-saver in centering designs within a field.

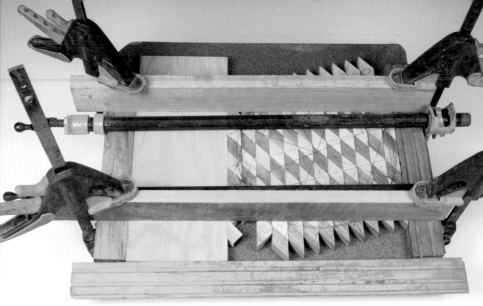

Our diamond design lazy susan in clamps and glue. Because of its unique shape, imaginative clamping is needed.

TIPS: Clamping the top of the glue-up jig to maintain flatness is just as important as clamping end-to-end to prevent gaps between segments. If we are not careful through the process to maintain flatness, our final project will be thinner than expected after planing or sanding.

Because of its unique shape, an imaginative use of clamps is necessary. Clamping the top to maintain flatness is just as important as clamping end-to-end to prevent gaps between segments.

Rip jigs are among my favorites to use, especially with odd shapes such as this one. If the jig is passed through the saw blade and a sixteenth or so is ripped off prior to mounting the odd shape, then as long as the rip fence is not moved or bumped, we can be assured that the edge of our jig board will align with the blade. Placing your odd shape is as simple as aligning your shape lines with the edge of the jig board and relocating your hold-down clamps to accommodate your shape.

Rip jigs are among my favorites for cutting odd shapes such as this octagonal.

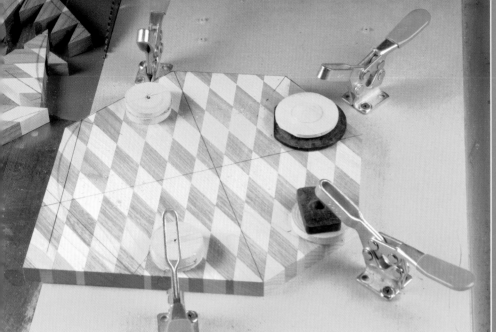

Use rubber and wooden spacers with the hold-down clamps to secure the odd shape to the jig board firmly.

Hold-down clamps used together with rubber and wooden spacers firmly secure the unusual octogon shape to our jig board. The hardware for this lazy susan can be found at any big-box store or online and comes with instructions for easy installation. The diamond design on this lazy susan looks great. It does not necessarily need an accent, or border, so I soften the edges with a router, sand, finish, and install the hardware.

The Herringbone Platter:
a 1"-180°-FS/1"-45°-HB Design

The herringbone pattern is easily achieved by flipping every other segment over and aligning the design. With this pattern, each segment of walnut meets with a birch segment, and each segment of birch meets a walnut one. This alternating light and dark design is a personal favorite and very catchy to the eye.

Once again, great care is taken with a magnifying glass to ensure our pattern is as close to perfect as possible. Once it is aligned properly, lines are drawn and markings made so that getting it back into precise position during glue-up is simple.

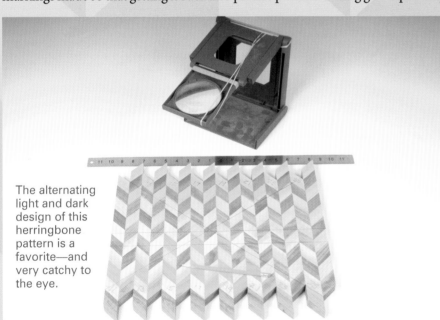

The alternating light and dark design of this herringbone pattern is a favorite—and very catchy to the eye.

APPLICATIONS:

Lazy susans are among my favorite projects because they can easily be personalized according to the woodworker's taste. Excess diamond material could be glued into turning blanks and fashioned on a lathe into salt and pepper shakers or grinding mills. Another popular accessory is the center napkin holder made from matching material, as seen on page 37.

Our herringbone platter in glue and clamps.

Maintaining flatness by vertically clamping is just as important as horizontally clamping end-to-end. Since most platters are rectangular, we will be using a rectangular shape. Once again a rip jig makes safe and easy work of these otherwise difficult cuts.

Rip jigs make this difficult cut safe and easy.

The jig is no longer necessary once we have a clean, square 90° edge to place against our rip fence.

The jig is no longer necessary once we have one straight edge at 180° and one square, 90° edge. The rip fence is used to clean up the edges with the help of these push blocks for flat surfaces. The pointed, sharp screws in the bottom of the push blocks help control the piece throughout the cut.

TIPS: When using these push blocks with drywall screws, be sure that the points of the screws do not descend below the bottom of the block more than needed to hold the board firmly in place. If your points are too long, you will create excess work for yourself by sanding out the dimple holes the screws leave behind.

The pointed, sharp screws in the bottom of the push blocks help control the piece throughout the cut. A square is used to ensure a 90° cut.

Bordering this platter with an accenting third color will really make the design stand out, so I have chosen to use cherry. The deep brown cherry will give the piece a framing effect and highlight the interior design. The border will also help protect the edges from any fragmentation of the smaller, more vulnerable pieces. Since the running grain of the border will be glued to the random grain of the design, there is no reason *not* to use a spline along all the edges to ensure the bordering cherry holds the design firmly in place.

Installing a spline is a simple process that ensures your project will hold together for years of use. Spline material can be purchased, along with biscuits and dowels (used in furniture-making), from any local hardware or big-box store. I prefer to custom-make splines from a premium grade of plywood or specialized floor underlayment material. For me, quarter-inch BC plywood works well and can be purchased in 2' x 2' pieces, making it very affordable. With the quarter-inch-wide spline, it is not necessary to use specialized dado blades. A standard blade cutting on either side of the center will usually make enough room for a good fit. It is important that the fit is not too tight; a comfortable friction while sliding the spline within its groove is sufficient. Splines can also be made from non-plywood material and sometimes serve as an accent when shown on the exterior edges of a piece.

All the parts for my spline are in place. Before gluing the spline, I will rip off half-inch sections of the cherry end pieces. These will act as caps in the final glue-up. This cap will hide top and bottom channel marks and the splines located at the board ends. I mark my caps so that when they are glued on, I can align the grain, making the glue lines less visible.

Our first border glue-ups are the ends from which we cut off our end caps. Take care to maintain your flatness across your design and into your border. A minimum of clamping pressure is needed here—just enough to hold them snugly in place. These ends are then trimmed with a rip jig to become flush with the bottom and top edges of the design.

All the parts needed to complete our platter.

Our first border glue-up. A light clamping pressure is all that is needed.

The side borders are glued in place with their splines.

The side borders are attached with their splines and trimmed with the rip jig so that the edges are even with the end borders.

Finally, our end caps are matched up with their original grain and are designed to cover our remaining spline and groove ends for a wonderful finished look.

Because the glue lines of the caps are hidden, we have the impression of masterful joinery with the added benefit of spline construction. This is a wonderful combination that will last for many years.

The caps are aligned in the final glue-up for this project.

Our grain alignment helps hide our glue lines, along with any indication of our spline and its groove.

Our lazy susan and platter before finishing.

Both our projects are ready for a standard finish of three to four coats of sanding sealer and a wipe-on poly.

Our completed diamond, walnut-and-birch lazy susan: 1"-180°-FS/1"-45°-DM.

Our completed herringbone platter: 1"-180°-FS/1"-45°-HB.

A close-up of the platter: the magnifying glass helped to ensure a tightly designed look when seen up close.

To help us visualize the characteristics of wood color and grain, I have created a similar diamond-pattern lazy susan and herringbone platter out of oak and cherry wood. Notice there is a much more subtle difference between the oak and cherry, as opposed to the distinct contrast of the walnut and birch. Both have an elegant beauty all their own.

TIPS: I love to use sapwood in my projects. Sapwood is the wood furthest from the center of the tree and close to the bark. It usually displays the transition from darker heartwood to the lighter, softer sapwood. Most woodworkers avoid or discard this distinctive material, but I find it sometimes can add wonderful accents. Notice the end border boards, which move from heartwood to sapwood in what I consider a dramatic display.

Another 1"-180°-FS/1"-45°-HB platter made of oak and a lighter cherry, with a walnut border. Notice the lighter contrast of the design, which gives the pattern a more modest, less outspoken, look.

A close-up of the oak and light cherry platter.

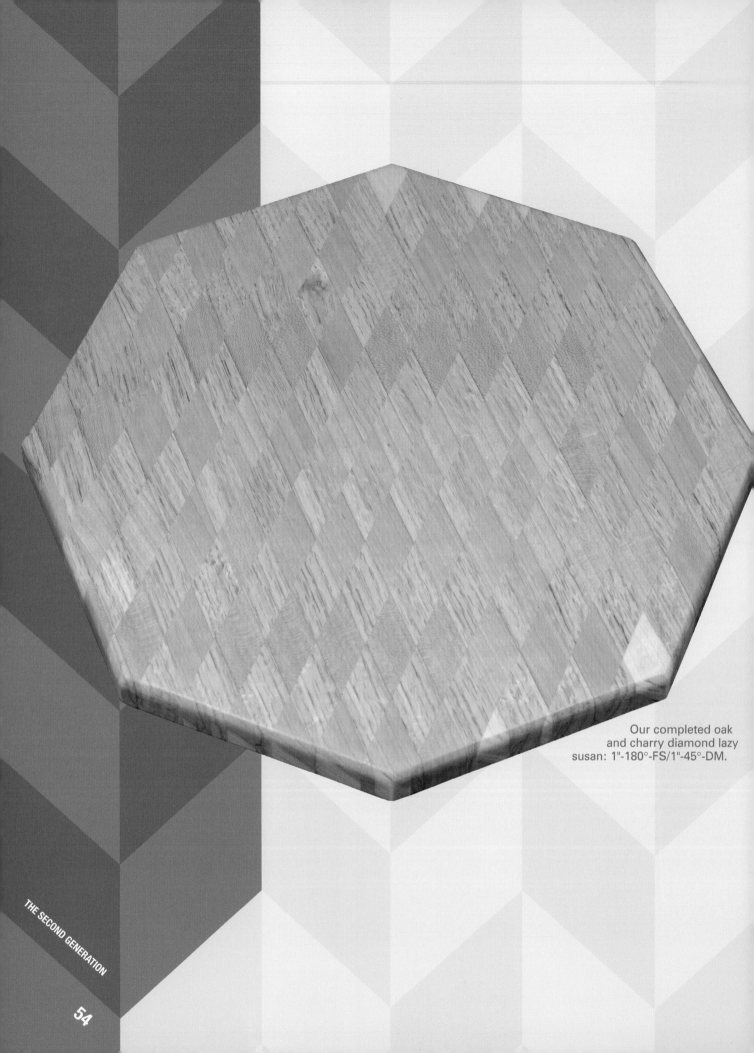

Our completed oak
and charry diamond lazy
susan: 1"-180°-FS/1"-45°-DM.

A close-up of both lazy susans (1"-180°-FS/1"-45°-DM) helps us compare a sharp contrast of colors and variation in available grain patterns.

VARIATIONS: Notice that the contrast in the oak-and-cherry lazy susan is comprised of wood grain more than color. The walnut-and-birch lazy susan on the other hand, enjoys a contrast of color more than wood grain. Combining color and grain contrast to highlight your artistic goals is a fun and exciting process.

Our lazy susans, side by side.

Defining Generational Designs

Before we proceed into the third generation, it is important that we have a deeper understanding of generational designs and how they are defined. Defining generational designs for the purposes of categorization and duplication is simple. We always begin with a board and then apply four major elements to it, creating a new board with a new display.

These four major elements are:

1 **Cut Location:** The location within the design or board where the cut is to be located;
2 **Degree Used:** The degree used in the cut;
3 **Intended Design:** The intended design created by combining the cut strips;
4 **Cut and Glue-Up:** The cut and subsequent glue-up of a new board, with the new design symbolized by a forward slash, or "/".

All that precedes the forward slash defines the cut to the board and how its segments are glued back together. A new board with a new design is created between each forward slash, allowing us to begin the process again.

A first-generation single stripe bordered by planks.
This linear lamination is termed a 180-1S.

For example, the board above is considered a 180°-1S. It consists of a single stripe bordered by planks. When the "Full" of the term "Full-Stripe" is substituted by a number, it not only implies the number of stripes employed but also the presence of "planks," or bordering pieces. These planks give a framing effect to the design with each generation, in this case the lighter wood surrounding the darker stripe. Let's now take this board, cut it up, and harvest the new segments into a new 180°-1S/1"-45°-CV board.

Cut locations are laid out every inch
along the length of the board.

Cut location: In our diagram above, note that cuts are applied every inch to our 180°-1S/ board, thus adding the 1" to our 180°-1S/1" designation. The 1 preceding the degree tells us where the cut is located. In this case the cut is located every inch along the length of the board.

TIPS: SketchUp® is a 3d modeling software program. I find this software to have great value in the design and experimentation stages of multi-generational projects.

On my website www.WoodArt.Biz, you will find a "downloads" page with access to SketchUp® files I have created including the diagrams found in this book. These files can easily be opened once you install the software through the internet, and they're free. Change them, reconfigure, and add additional generations to them.

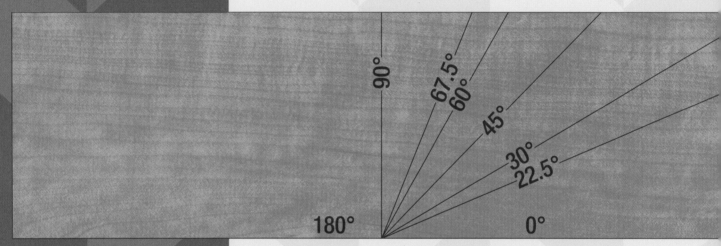

45° cuts are applied every inch along the board.

The Degree Used: The degree is a description of what angle is used to cut through our 180°-1S/1" board and is located directly after the cut location, or 180°-1S/1"-45° in our example. We know it will be every inch along the length as seen above, and we now know that the cut applied will be 45°.

Degrees can be tricky because shop equipment, such as table saws, miters, and chop boxes, utilize degree markings that may not conform to a 180° linear orientation to our board. For our purposes, all degree calculations will be oriented to the material's linear lamination, or the 0° to 180° standard rip cut, along the length of the material running with the grain of the wood. When I am standing at my table saw, I am located at 180°, facing through the blade at the 0° mark at the far side of the table saw blade.

Table saws, miters, and chop boxes utilize degree markings that may not conform to the 180° linear orientation of our board.

As seen above, to cut that material in half (a cross-cut) would be a 90° cut. A 60° cut would be lower off that 90° cut. A 45° cut would be located below that and is usually the sharpest cut permitted by most miter boxes and table saw miter gages. Things get more challenging when cutting below 45°. Specialized jigs make this easier, but most standard equipment is not made to handle cuts below 45°, so care and caution are required. That being said, the more dramatic the angle, the sharper the contrast and the design it yields. I have made cuts at 22.5°, which I would recommend only to the experienced. Cuts at 30° are popular for the multi-generational process, but a specialized jig and care are required in its use.

The Intended Design: The intended design is the application of the cut pieces into a new board with a new pattern or design. What will this new board, which we have created from harvested one-inch, 45° segments, look like? Potential designs are limitless, but some common examples include the following:

Abbreviations

FS	Full-Stripe
#S	The number of stripes followed by the S for stripe implies the use of planks, or in this case the bordering, lighter colored wood surrounding our single darker stripe.
DM	Diamond
HB	Herringbone
CV	Chevron
CB	Checker board. Half-steps utilize the .5 designation.

Every other segment is turned over to create a chevron design.

As seen above, by turning every other segment over we create a chevron design. This chevron design is noted with a CV and is located after our degree marking, or 180°-1S/1"-45°-CV/.

It is important, especially during the foundational first and second generations, to clearly label the recipe used and the patterns formed. By the third generation and beyond, it becomes increasingly difficult to spot in the design where you started.

The Cut and Glue-up: The cut and subsequent glue-up of the new board with its new design is symbolized by the forward slash, /. This forward slash represents the creation of a new board using the specifications of that which precedes it, with the glue dried and the clamps removed, ready for the next set of specifications. Our 180°-1S/1"-45°-CV/ specification tells us that we created one board with a single stripe (180°-1S), and then harvested from it the segments used to create a second board with a chevron design (1"-45°-CV). Further, the forward slash at the end tells me we are now ready to harvest from that new board the parts needed to create our third generation.

An example of this process can be seen in our Platter in Chapter 6 (page 52), a 1"-180°-FS/1"-45°-HB/:

First Generation: 1" cuts at 180° are made. The new segments are glued back into a full-stripe board form.

Second Generation: 1" cuts at 45° are made. The new segments are glued back into a herringbone pattern.

Our completed herringbone platter: 1"-180°-FS/1"-45°-HB

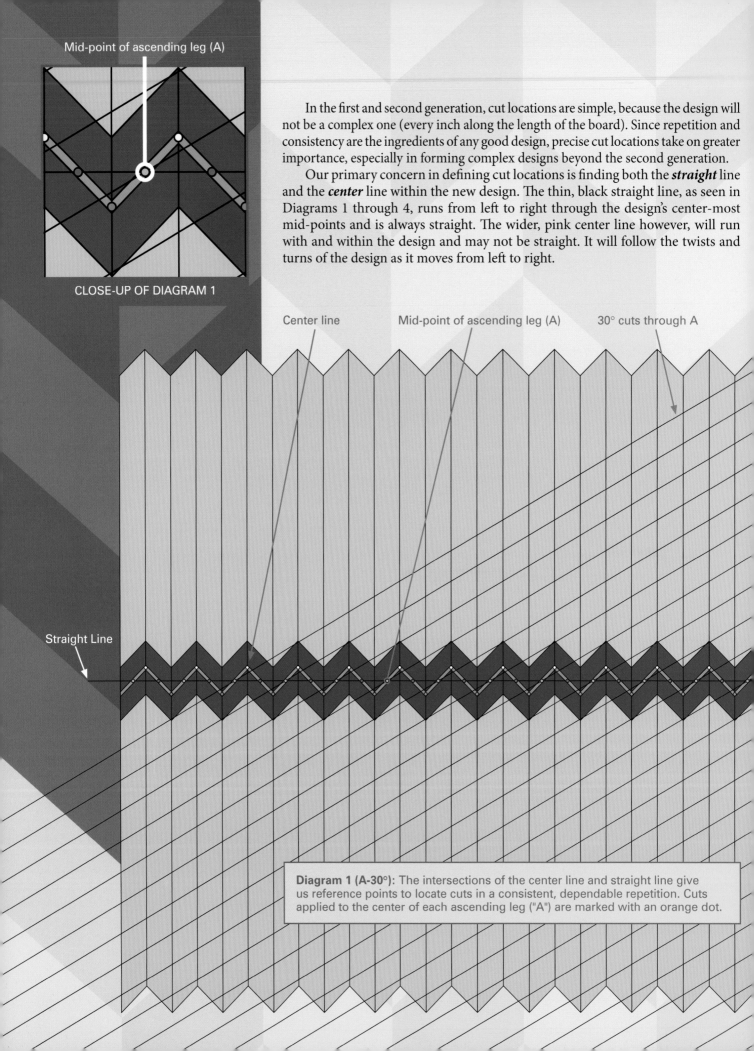

Mid-point of ascending leg (A)

CLOSE-UP OF DIAGRAM 1

In the first and second generation, cut locations are simple, because the design will not be a complex one (every inch along the length of the board). Since repetition and consistency are the ingredients of any good design, precise cut locations take on greater importance, especially in forming complex designs beyond the second generation.

Our primary concern in defining cut locations is finding both the *straight* line and the *center* line within the new design. The thin, black straight line, as seen in Diagrams 1 through 4, runs from left to right through the design's center-most mid-points and is always straight. The wider, pink center line however, will run with and within the design and may not be straight. It will follow the twists and turns of the design as it moves from left to right.

Center line

Mid-point of ascending leg (A)

30° cuts through A

Straight Line

Diagram 1 (A-30°): The intersections of the center line and straight line give us reference points to locate cuts in a consistent, dependable repetition. Cuts applied to the center of each ascending leg ("A") are marked with an orange dot.

If we have an even number of stripes, our center line will be the glue line between the two center-most stripes as it zigzags through the design from left to right. An odd number of stripes, including a single stripe (as seen in these diagrams), will give us a center line in the center of the middle (only) stripe, zigzagging through the chevrons from left to right. The intersections of the thin straight line and the pink center line give us reference points to locate cuts in a consistent, dependable repetition.

When we read the design along its center line from left to right, we note that some of the legs of that center line are ascending and some descending. A cut location at the center of each ascending leg (marked with an orange dot, as seen in Diagram 1) is termed "A." The location at the center of each descending leg (represented by a blue dot, as seen in Diagram 2) is termed "D."

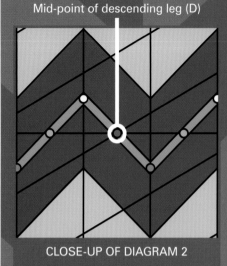

Mid-point of descending leg (D)

CLOSE-UP OF DIAGRAM 2

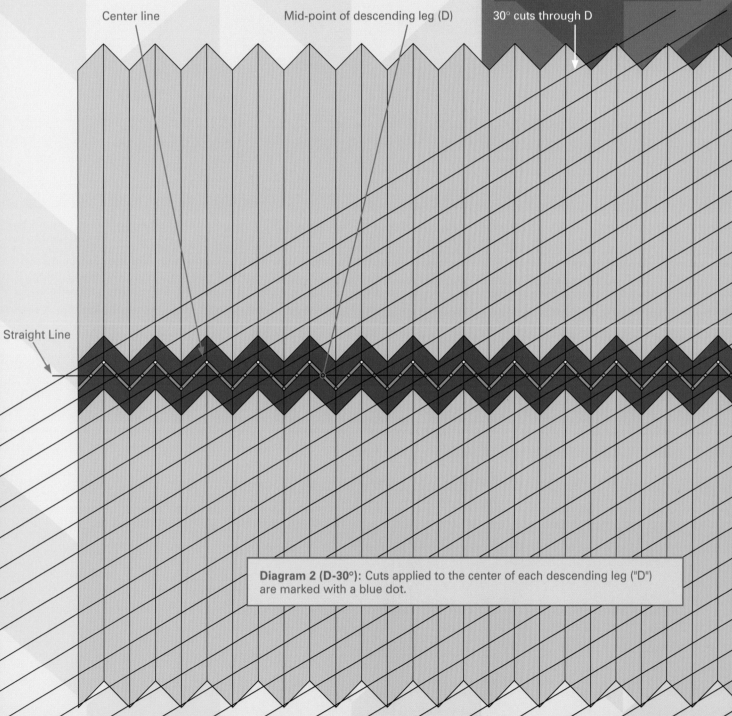

Center line

Mid-point of descending leg (D)

30° cuts through D

Straight Line

Diagram 2 (D-30°): Cuts applied to the center of each descending leg ("D") are marked with a blue dot.

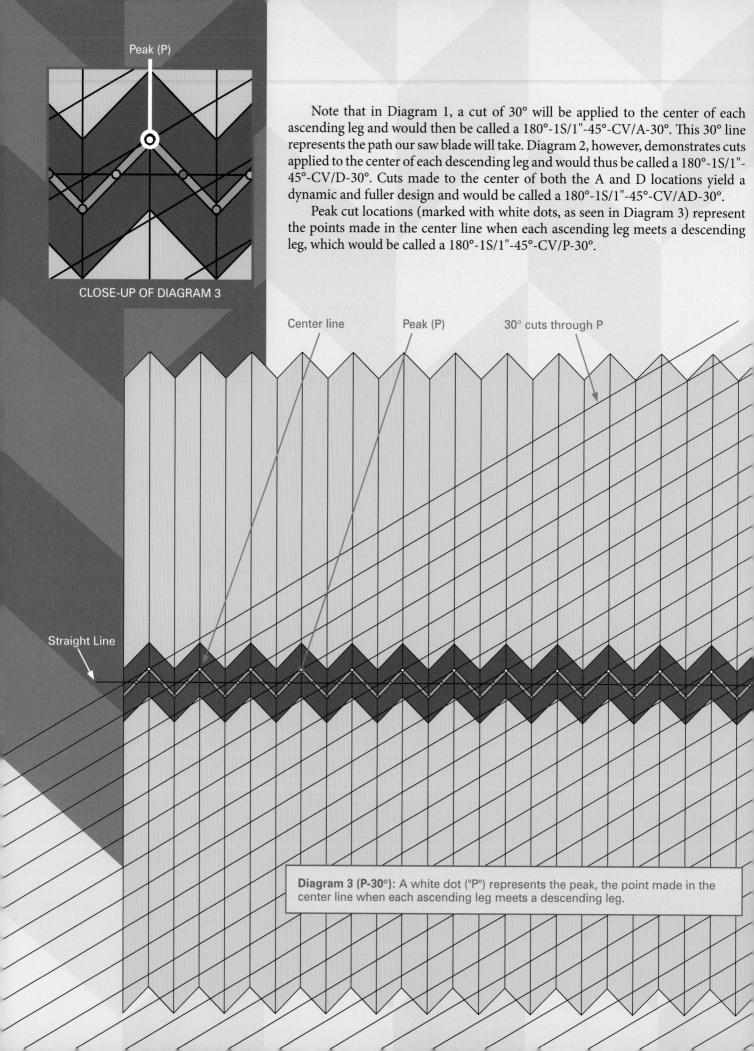

Peak (P)

CLOSE-UP OF DIAGRAM 3

Note that in Diagram 1, a cut of 30° will be applied to the center of each ascending leg and would then be called a 180°-1S/1"-45°-CV/A-30°. This 30° line represents the path our saw blade will take. Diagram 2, however, demonstrates cuts applied to the center of each descending leg and would thus be called a 180°-1S/1"-45°-CV/D-30°. Cuts made to the center of both the A and D locations yield a dynamic and fuller design and would be called a 180°-1S/1"-45°-CV/AD-30°.

Peak cut locations (marked with white dots, as seen in Diagram 3) represent the points made in the center line when each ascending leg meets a descending leg, which would be called a 180°-1S/1"-45°-CV/P-30°.

Center line   Peak (P)   30° cuts through P

Straight Line

Diagram 3 (P-30°): A white dot ("P") represents the peak, the point made in the center line when each ascending leg meets a descending leg.

The trough, or valley, created when each descending leg meets an ascending one (marked with a green dot, as seen in Diagram 4) would be termed a 180°-1S/1"-45°-CV/T-30°. These cut locations can be used together or separately, depending on the desired effect or intended design.

Although these defining characteristics vary, this gives us a starting point to classify and duplicate our work. With this simple design legend, we can map out and sketch many complex patterns.

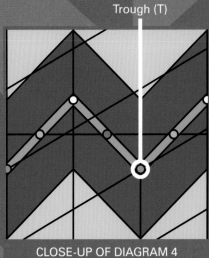

Trough (T)

CLOSE-UP OF DIAGRAM 4

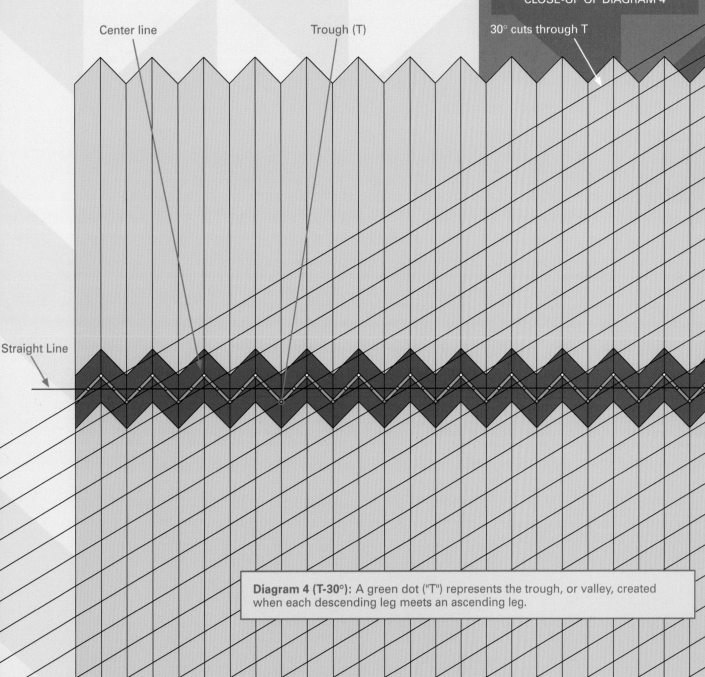

Center line

Trough (T)

30° cuts through T

Straight Line

Diagram 4 (T-30°): A green dot ("T") represents the trough, or valley, created when each descending leg meets an ascending leg.

The Third Generation

Applying a 60° Cut to Points A and D

With our third-generation lamination, we will be creating two cutting boards, one of walnut and birch, and one of oak and cherry. Our walnut and birch material will become a 1"-180°-FS/1"-45°-CV/D-60°/ and our cherry and oak material will become a 1"-180°-FS/1"-45°-CV/A-60°/. Note that the only difference between our two boards will be their material (oak and cherry v. walnut and birch) and their cut locations (D-60° v. A-60°).

We begin our third-generation lamination with the same material we have created in Chapter 5, a 1"-180°-FS/1"-45°. In the photo below, we see both the cherry and oak (top) and the walnut and birch (bottom). From here we will depart from the projects of Chapter 6 by applying a chevron design (CV) made from our 45° strips, creating a zigzag pattern.

The building blocks of our third-generation design, in both the cherry and oak (top) and the walnut and birch (bottom).

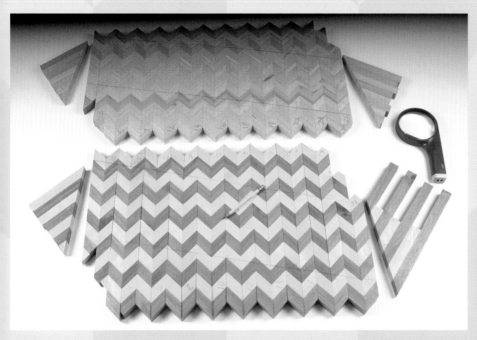

Use a magnifying glass to align the design precisely before glue-up; draw lines to make realignment easier when gluing.

Third-Generation Cutting Board

Walnut and Birch – 1"-180°-FS/1"-45°-CV/D-60°/

Our clamps are ready, and glue is poured out to the right of our table top to dunk our 45° segments, creating the second of our three generations.

Glue is applied to our 45° pieces.

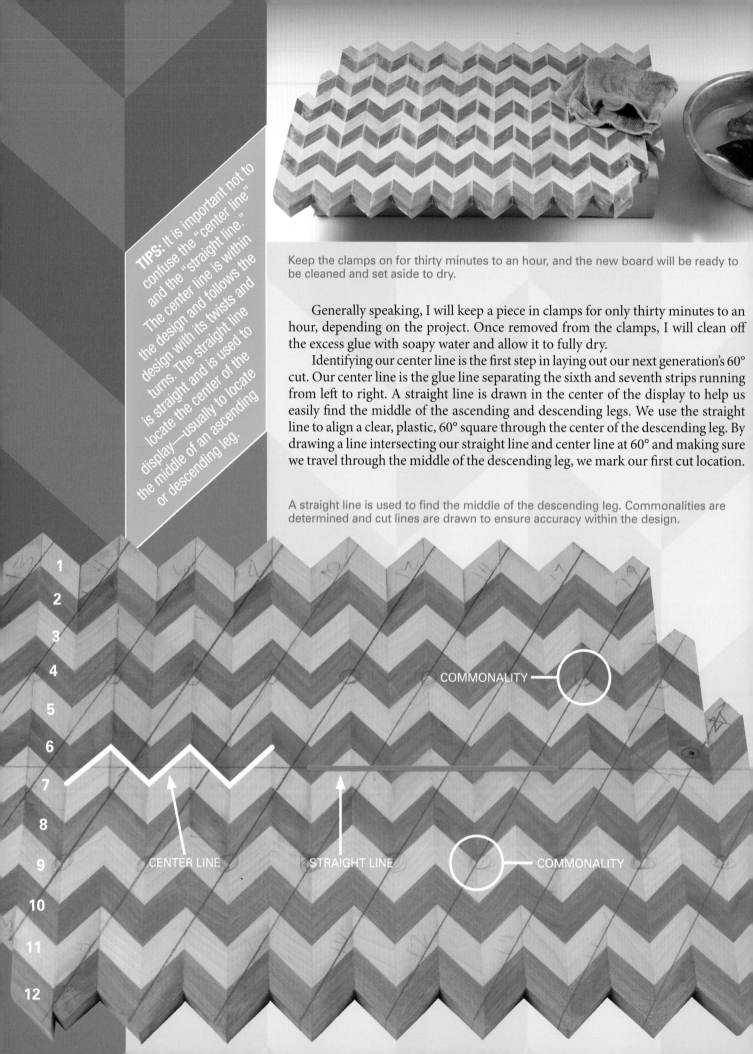

Keep the clamps on for thirty minutes to an hour, and the new board will be ready to be cleaned and set aside to dry.

Generally speaking, I will keep a piece in clamps for only thirty minutes to an hour, depending on the project. Once removed from the clamps, I will clean off the excess glue with soapy water and allow it to fully dry.

Identifying our center line is the first step in laying out our next generation's 60° cut. Our center line is the glue line separating the sixth and seventh strips running from left to right. A straight line is drawn in the center of the display to help us easily find the middle of the ascending and descending legs. We use the straight line to align a clear, plastic, 60° square through the center of the descending leg. By drawing a line intersecting our straight line and center line at 60° and making sure we travel through the middle of the descending leg, we mark our first cut location.

A straight line is used to find the middle of the descending leg. Commonalities are determined and cut lines are drawn to ensure accuracy within the design.

1
2
3
4
5
6
7
8
9
10
11
12

COMMONALITY

CENTER LINE   STRAIGHT LINE   COMMONALITY

Within that first 60° pencil mark, we notice *commonalities*. A commonality is an intersecting point between the design and our 60° line, which will be common to all our 60° markings. Watching how the line interacts with the design, ascending at 60° from bottom to top and left to right, we notice where it intersects with points within the design. I see that the 60° marking intersects with the troughs of stripes 8 and 9 and the peaks of stripes 4 and 5, for example (as shown on page 66, circled in white), which I circle in pencil.

Rather than drawing my 60° lines using our clear, plastic 60° square, I allow these points to become my focus for drawing my cut markings. The design—its tightness and uniformity—is the primary concern; using the design to define the cut marks helps ensure greater uniformity in the display.

With our rip fence firmly in position, our jig's edge is first run through the table saw so that we can be certain that any alignment with the jig's edge will also align with the blade. Using a small square, we mark the cut lines with a pencil on the surface of the chevron board and down both the front and rear edges of the chevron, aligning those marks with the jig's edge. With help from the penciled-in lines, we know if our cutting is accurate by watching the blade pass along that line as closely as possible during the cut.

ALIGN EDGE WITH PENCIL MARK

ALIGN EDGE WITH PENCIL MARK

The lines are brought to the bottom of the chevron board so they can be lined up with the edge of the jig.

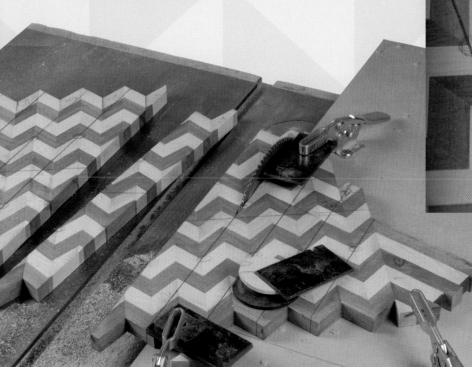

With the rip fence firmly in position, a ripping jig makes these difficult cuts accurate, safe, and easy.

TIPS: The "saw kerf" (material removed by the saw blade after a cut that is turned into sawdust) can affect a design. Cuts to the left of your penciled line will produce a display different from those positioned to the right or middle of your penciled cut line. Consistency is the primary objective. Cutting in the same location relative to your penciled lines will give you a more uniform display and better looking design.

VARIATIONS: Typical third and fourth generations utilize a pattern formed by flipping over, and/or end-for-end, every other segment. There is a world of variations on this theme and variations on those patterns. Flipping end-for-end, turning every other one over, or just aligning to a different point in the design are all good methods of finding new designs. Experimentation in alignment of the segments is a fun and exciting process.

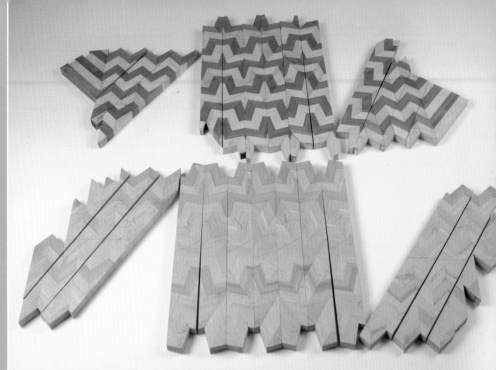

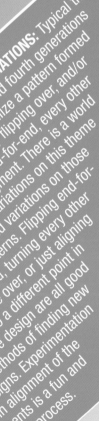

Our cut boards with every other segment flipped over.

Above, our designs begin to take shape. By flipping over every other one, our patterns emerge. With magnifying glass in hand, we align our design to make the most appealing display possible.

Again, use a magnifying glass to create the most appealing display possible.

Our 1"-180°-FS/1"-45°-CV/D-60° design after the glue-up.

After the glue-up, our walnut-and-birch cutting board begins to take shape. By drawing potential shapes on our material, we recognize which ones augment the design pattern and allow us to maximize our material. For this cutting board I have chosen a parallelogram.

Shapes are drawn on the surface to determine the best use of our material—a parallelogram is chosen.

HEADS UP: If your saw blade seems to "drift" off your penciled cut lines during your cut, this may be an indication that your material is moving on your jig surface. This can cause dangerous kickbacks and damage your material and saw blades. Be sure your work piece is secured firmly to your jig surface with hold-down clamps and peal-and-stick sand paper, so that the jig and the material clamped to it always move as one.

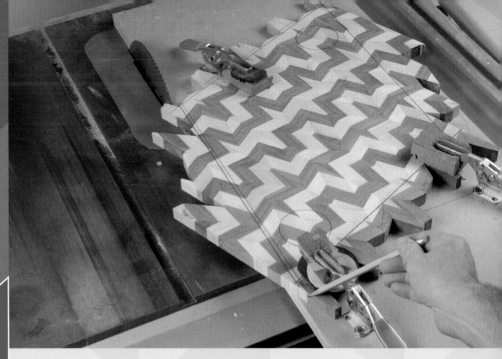

Back to our ripping jig to trim our board to the desired shape.

A ripping jig once again makes safe and easy cuts by aligning the pencil marks with the edge of the jig. After cutting our shape, we see that not much material is wasted. A hole saw makes quick work of handle holds on either end. A router is used to soften and slightly round the edges.

HEADS UP: When using a hole saw, it is important to begin with a pilot hole all the way through your material. Then apply your hole saw equally from both sides to the center. Hole saws tend to tear out the bottom, ripping some of the surface of the underside, if allowed to go completely through the material in one pass.

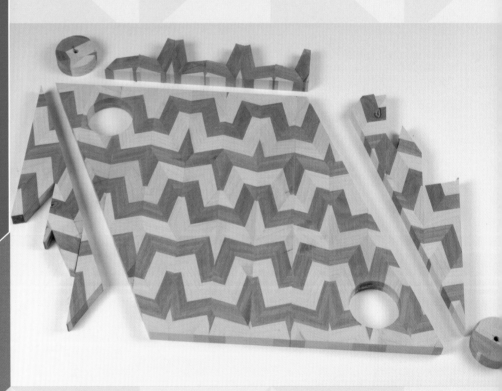

Not much wasted with this shape; our Parallelogram cutting board begins to take shape.

Our finished
cutting board

CUMULATIVE ERROR

An up-close view reveals both
the highlights and the presence of
cumulative error.

The unique shape of our cutting board—matched by the sharp, pointed design—make this conversation piece a one-of-a-kind addition to any kitchen. A close-up view of our cutting board reveals a number of things: first, the unique way the crisscrossing grain and contrast in wood color highlight and draw the eye into the design; secondly, it is important to recognize the effects of cumulative error within our work. With each generation, imperfections are magnified, becoming more noticeable.

Even with our careful and deliberate cutting (entering and exiting the design at precise points), imperfections can be seen. I feel these variations are within acceptable limits. However, a fourth generation would reveal very noticeable and unsightly discrepancies in pattern and design. I would not attempt a fourth generation without beginning again from the first generation and moving all the way through the process with greater care.

Third-Generation Cutting Board
– Cherry and Oak –
1"-180°-FS/1"-45°-CV/A-60°/

Our cherry and oak cutting board is laid out for a 60° cut to the ascending leg of the center line. First, the center line is located. Second, a straight line is drawn to locate the middle of the ascending leg. Third, a 60°, clear plastic square helps us draw our first 60° line in relation to our straight line, through that ascending leg. A quick examination reveals commonalities located on the peak of the 2nd and 3rd stripe and the trough of the 10th and 11th stripe. These commonalities give us design-consistent cut lines to mark and follow during cutting.

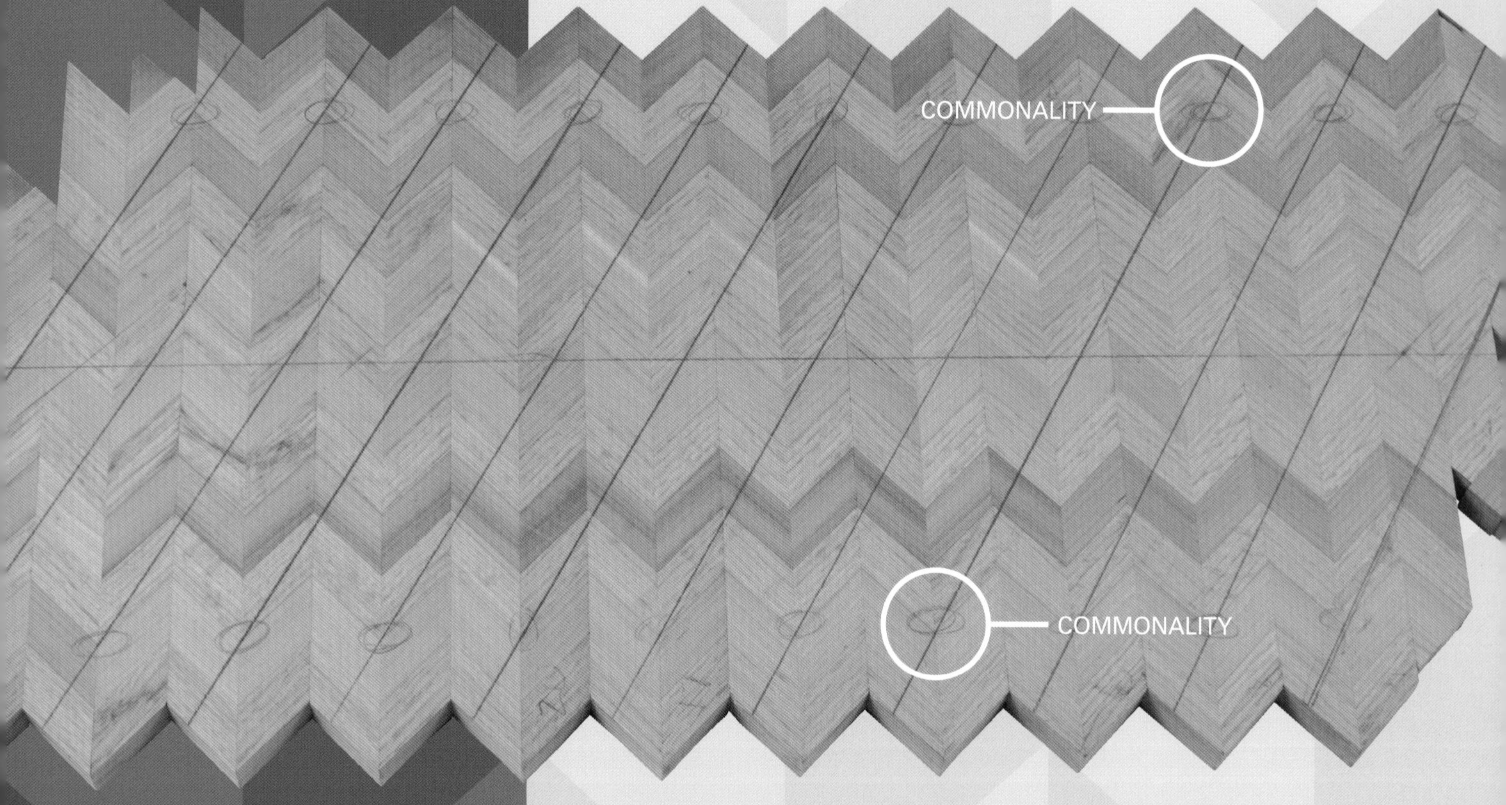

COMMONALITY

COMMONALITY

Our cherry and oak board will receive an A-60° cut, creating a 1"-180°-FS/1"-45°-CV/A-60°.

ALIGN PENCIL MARK WITH EDGE OF JIG →

Again, the pencil line is oriented to the jig edge.

The edge of the jig shows us where the blade will cut, so it is a simple matter of lining up the pencil line with the jig edge. Clamping your material securely to the jig with hold-down clamps is essential as you pass the work piece through the blade.

Our cherry and oak cutting board is aligned to give us the best design presentation possible. Every other segment is flipped end to end, creating this dynamic display. With the help of my magnifying glass, the segments are aligned as accurately as possible.

Our cherry and oak cutting board is examined.

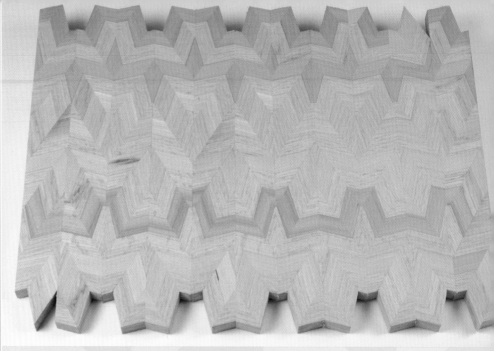

Out of the glue-up jig and ready for trimming and handles.

Once our board is out of the glue-up jig, it is examined, and potential shapes are drawn. One shape I tend to enjoy is that of the design itself. Since the design edges are the same as the shape edges, this unique look is distinctive and very original. Ordinarily, I might trim these edges straight and finish with a border material (like our herringbone platter in Chapter 6, with splines). Instead, I have opted for the toothy look of our design for a shape that complements and follows the design itself.

This method requires a lot more work to sand, because it becomes necessary to sand between each of the teeth, but I feel the extra work is a small price to pay for the distinctiveness of this classy display.

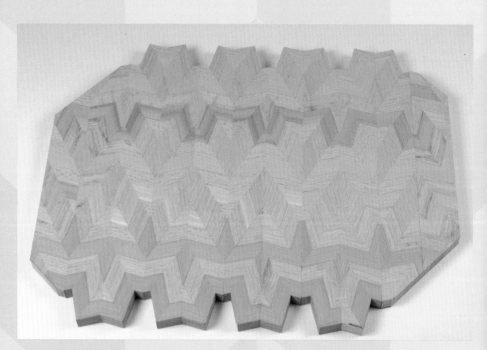

I like the way the shape follows the contours of the design, so I decided to leave these "teeth," where ordinarily I might trim them off.

TIPS: It is important to remember that excess glue is very difficult to sand off or remove after it is dried. If later I decide to use the design shape without trimming, it may cause trouble if I have not cleaned the glue off completely. I use a toothbrush to keep the "teeth" along the edges clear of glue squeeze-out before it dries on all my projects. As a result, I always have the option to use the unique design shapes along the edges, if I choose to do so.

TIPS: These "teeth" can be difficult to sand. I use strips of old sanding belts of varying widths, much like dental floss. The back and forth motion makes getting in the nooks and crannies much easier.

Handles are constructed using a hole saw and jig saw.

Use a hole saw and jig saw to create handles. The hole saw cuts circles in pre-positioned locations, and the jig saw is used to remove the material between those holes. A router is used to round and soften all the edges.

APPLICATIONS: With each successive generation, our material grows wider. With the multi-generational, method we are always substituting length of a board for its width. This factor tends to make these third and fourth generation projects wider, and as such, perfect candidates for table tops, end tables, and coffee tables. Bordering material of the same wood in a first- or second-generation display can be added with a spline along the edges, which makes these designs really pop.

Our finished cutting board.

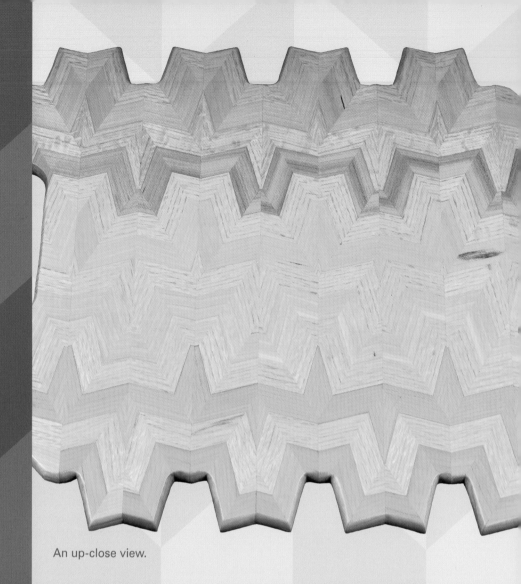
An up-close view.

Once again, an up-close view reveals a number of things: first, the contrast is diminished with the cherry and oak, compared to the walnut and birch. This more modest, less distinctive color display gives the piece a warmer sensibility. Some of the cherry strips are darker, giving the piece a framed look. As the middle cherry is lighter—nearly the same color as the oak—it highlights the grain pattern and rewards those who take a closer look with distinctive twists and turns of grain. All in all, I am thrilled with the result. Secondly, examining the pattern for tightness and uniformity of design shows few imperfections, as there is less variation in the pattern. With cumulative error at a lower level and fewer noticeable imperfections in design than our walnut-and-birch cutting board, I would feel very comfortable moving forward with a fourth or even a fifth generation.

CHAPTER 8

THE NOT-SO-LAZY SUSAN
A Case Study

This lazy susan is a wonderful piece I call "Not-So-Lazy Susan." It is a basic progression of generational laminations using walnut and maple, beginning with our familiar 1"-180°-FS.

"Not-So-Lazy Susan" is a basic progression of generational laminations.

Our recipe for this project is: 1"-180°-FS/1"-60°-CV/D-45°/D-60°. Note that we are using four generations, so care must be taken with every cut and each glue-up to prevent cumulative error. A magnifying glass and attention to detail are a must.

First generation: We begin with our familiar 1"-180°-FS. In this case, eight strips of walnut and maple cut to a one-inch width are used to create a striped board approximately four feet in length.

Second generation: 1"-60°-CV. Our board is cut into one-inch strips at 60° and reconstructed into a chevron (CV) or zigzag pattern.

Third generation: D-45°. For this lamination, we take our chevron board and locate the descending leg of the center line. Making cuts to the center of each descending leg at 45°, we reconstruct our board.

Fourth generation: To that board, we apply our fourth and final lamination by locating the center line within the new design, and apply 60° cuts to the center of each of its descending legs. This new design material is reconstructed into what you see below.

Trimming out our shape is simple, and a mahogany border is applied with splines for added strength and stability for years of use. The twists and turns of the design highlight the pointed and eye-catching pattern, along with the contrast in wood color.

The twists and turns of this design give it a commanding and bold look.

As stated in the introduction: "All the concepts and projects in this book are simple. They may not be easy (some are more so than others), but they are all simple. What is the difference, you may ask, between the 'simple' and the 'easy?' Oh, about two or three tries."

The "Not-So-Lazy Susan" case study may look complex and difficult, but it's actually simple. If you are willing to work through the generations and the steps, it is absolutely achievable and doable. My first-generational woodworking projects were confined to one and two laminations. Only after I began getting consistent results did I feel confident enough to move forward into third- and fourth-generation laminations. As your skills grow and your confidence with jigs increases, the world of multiple generations begins to open wide.

I was first introduced to the multi-generational method through Malcomb Tibbets work *The Art of Segmented Wood Turning*, a must-have for anyone with a lathe. However, I also enjoy flat work and was looking for something off the lathe.

Clarence Rennefeld's work *Laminated Designs In Wood* was an eye-opener, and helped me to take this expressive art form and use it across a variety of applications. Although his book is out of print, it is a must-have for anyone looking for the next level in generational design.

Lastly, I would like to thank you, the reader, for your interest in the multi-generational method. I would like to ask you to reach out to me through my website, www.WoodArt.biz, and directly at Steve@WoodArt.biz, with pictures of your projects and comments on how you may have found this book helpful. I look forward to hearing from you!

PARTING SHOTS AND
FURTHER READING